BRAZILIAN FOOD

Felipe Castanho

Seu Chicão

Felipe Rameh

Janaina & Jefferson
Rueda

Roberta Sudbrack

Leandro Batista

Marcelo Amaral

Rodrigo Oliveira

Júnior Durski

BRAZILIAN FOOD

BY THIAGO CASTANHO & LUCIANA BIANCHI

Thiago Castanho

Brazilian Food by Thiago Castanho and Luciana Bianchi

An Hachette UK Company
www.hachette.co.uk

First published in Great Britain in 2014 by Mitchell Beazley,
a division of Octopus Publishing Group Ltd,
Carmelite House, 50 Victoria Embankment,
London EC4Y 0DZ
www.octopusbooks.co.uk

This paperback edition published in 2016

Text by Thiago Castanho & Luciana Bianchi

Translation: Elisa D. Teixeira

Photography: Rogério Voltan, Bruno Regis & Luciana Bianchi

Food Styling: Luciana Bianchi

Publisher: Alison Starling

Senior Editor: Sybella Stephens

Copy Editor: Jenni Muir

Art Director: Jonathan Christie

Designer: Pene Parker

Senior Production Manager: Katherine Hockley

ISBN 978 1 78472 244 9

Printed in China

CONTENTS

MY BRAZILIAN CUISINE

An Amazonian perspective

Brazilian cuisine is a mystery to many people. Brazil is a vast country with many ethnic influences and climates and, just as any other place in the world, it has its iconic dishes and a variety of regional cuisines. To the north, we are blessed with 60 per cent of the Amazon rainforest, the world's lung within our territory. For most people it is a far-away land – for me, it is home!

The term 'Amazonian cuisine' can be applied to any dishes using Amazonian produce; however, in my country it also refers to the cuisine of the Amazon region, which is a state of Brazil. Pará, the area in which I live, is set in the Amazon rainforest and its cuisine is probably one of the most authentic in Brazil, with a strong base in the diet of native Brazilians. It is a terroir cuisine, using fruits, vegetables, herbs and roots from the forest, and fish and meat from the region.

There is no real winter here, so we have an abundance of fresh fruit and vegetables all year round. They have indigenous names, exotic flavours, powerful odours and unusual textures and include açaí, cupuaçu, bacuri, pupunha, tucumã, muruci, piquiá, taperebá and many others. Cassavas and yams are part of our staple diet, and come in various forms, served as vegetables and also providing various kinds of flour. Fish plays a central role in the cuisine of the Amazon, too; wild fish such as pirarucu, tucunaré and tambaqui feature on our menus daily, prepared not only in a traditional way, but also using a more contemporary approach.

Brazilian food is a diet full of protein, low in fat and very healthy. Many of our dishes can be successfully prepared without our indigenous or local produce. In this book the recipes use authentic Brazilian ingredients – however, I have also suggested a number of alternative ingredients that will be more easily available to enable you to 'cook Brazilian' using your local fish and vegetables. Many Brazilian foods can already be found in supermarkets around the world, including hearts of palm, the 'superfruit' açaí, mangoes, coconuts, cassava and plantains. Others, you will find in specialist Brazilian, Asian and African food shops, and may be purchased online, too. See page 251 for a list of suppliers to help you find the ingredients referred to in the recipes.

I will also introduce you to some of my friends from different regions of the country – people who are doing unique work, combining their love for traditional cuisine with a contemporary vision, and who have provided recipes for this book. You will also find some recipes created by people who are not chefs, but who often make dishes better than any professional – my mother being one of them.

I hope you enjoy *Brazilian Food*, preparing the recipes at home for your family and friends. My wish is that these pages will motivate you to visit Brazil soon to get to know our many culinary treasures and very welcoming people. Bom apetite!

A FAMILY STORY

It all started in 2000 when my father turned our living room into a small village restaurant. He was just cooking for the neighbours to begin with, but one by one, our living room furniture disappeared and we saw tables and chairs take their place. My dad was in the kitchen, preparing his favourite home-style dishes, and we were all helping –my mum, my young brother and me. I was only 11 and I remember seeing my dad in the kitchen and the hungry neighbours and guests waiting for his delicious food. As the years passed, our house became a kind of secret among food lovers – they even called it 'the secret restaurant'! We called it Remanso do Peixe, which can be translated as a 'quiet and relaxed fish place'. After eight years, the restaurant took over most of our house and we decided to move down the road. Remanso do Peixe was finally a restaurant of its own.

We received many national awards as the best fish restaurant in Brazil, but even today it looks like an ordinary family home. There is no sign at the door, no luxurious plates or furniture, only simple homemade food and no fuss.

At 12 years of age I was helping in the kitchen and fell in love with my father's job. I grew up, finished college and enrolled at university for a course on Informatics. However, my heart longed for the kitchen, and I decided to apply for a degree in gastronomy 3,000 kilometres away from home. I returned to my home city after completing the course, and entered my father's kitchen full of new ideas, little experience, but a lot of teenage confidence. Seu Chicão, as we all call my dad, gave me a valuable piece of advice: 'Before innovating, you need to know the basics. You need to get to know the products, talk to the producers and market vendors, and understand the culinary traditions of our region. Only after that will you be ready to innovate.'

In 2011 we opened our second restaurant, Remanso do Bosque (which translates as 'quiet place in the woods'). This is a proper restaurant and represents a new phase in our family life. Now we are innovating and keeping the traditions alive at the same time. We are investing in research, discovering new native products and hosting events with other chefs and food professionals. Remanso do Bosque is located in front of the Rodrigues Alves national park, part of the Amazon rainforest. We are privileged to have the largest and most important market in Latin America, Ver-o-Peso, only a few minutes from the restaurant, and we are 30 minutes from Combu Island where our homemade chocolate is made by Nena (see page 214). We care for and support all our suppliers, and they support us like a family.

My brother, Felipe, decided to go to the same school of gastronomy that I did and is now my right hand at Remanso do Bosque. My mother, Dona Carmem, is our office and finance manager. My father, Seu Chicão, is the foundation of this family business, and we still learn from him every day. This book is a culinary diary of our family story and we are very happy to share it with you.

WHAT IS BRAZILIAN FOOD?

CARLOS ALBERTO DÓRIA

Brazil is so vast and such a young nation that its cuisine is still a work in progress. You can always discover something new, as the nation's culinary talent lies in its ability to reinvent itself. This means that in the 21st century, apart from carnival and football, Brazil will be known for its gastronomy.

When I travel around the country and, once home, unpack my suitcases, I have numerous packets of flour and jars of fruit compote that are unknown to my own family, or indigenous ground dried chillies that I don't know either. Or tiny dried shrimps (called aviú) that are only found in the mouth of certain Amazonian rivers; beans of colours and shapes that amaze us – hundreds of varieties of the best beans – authentic and unique. When I go around the country, what strikes me is that I experience precisely the same spirit of discovery as when I travel abroad, getting to know new countries. But when chefs do the same thing, they don't just come back with a full suitcase, like a box of magic tricks: they come back with ideas that they put into practice, as we shall see throughout this book. We Brazilians are now discovering something that was always within arm's reach but which we didn't value in the way we do today: diversity. However, despite this overwhelming diversity we have built a familiar cuisine that any Brazilian, in all corners of the country, will know and appreciate. One based on feijoadas, moquecas of fish, prawns or crab, lavish barbecues, rice and beans, corn and cassava flours, bananas, mangoes, papaya and cashew fruit.

As I see Brazilian cuisine, we can identify two main categories that follow the historical lines of territorial conquest. In the Amazon and along the vast coast, right down to Rio Grande do Sul, cooked and stewed foods predominate and the table is laden with broths. In the countryside, which rises over the plateaus and lowlands of the borders with Argentina and Uruguay as far as the fringes of the Amazon, the dominant activity was cattle breeding. Here, the cuisine specializes in barbecues and beef jerky, and in dried foods mixed with flour. These could be eaten without being cooked over a fire or even without dismounting from a horse. In that way the difference between the coast and the interior is expressed in two families of dishes: the large family of moquecas and the family of paçocas and cuscuzes.

If the history of colonization has shaped these two main tendencies in our cooking, it also worked on a day-to-day basis, establishing differences according to what was available in each region and the particular traditions of the colonized and colonizers. Portuguese, African and native Indians had to find creative ways of contributing to the table, according to the 'fruitfulness of the land'. I can just imagine the Portuguese and Spaniards venturing deep into the Amazon rainforest, bumping into dozens of different indigenous peoples with different food preferences and with certain constants that proved irresistible to the settlers. Indeed, Brazilian cuisine grew out of the great convergence between different kinds of flour.

The settlers held out for as long as they could, guaranteeing the provision of wheat flour in the main cities of the coast. However, as they moved deeper into the forests and fields, with the ensuing difficulties in supply, they eventually bowed to the native Indians.

The shift that placed white cassava flour (named carimã) on an equal footing with wheat flour saw the 'European flour' replaced early on. Also, out of necessity, the colonizers gradually got used to the coarser cassava flours. And in the south and southeast of what is now Brazil, the Tupi-Guarani Indians used farinha de milho (a flaked cornmeal), which was imposed on the conquerors.

Since the 19th century, then, Brazil has been a country whose cuisine depends on three kinds of starch: the flour and meal derived from wheat, cassava and corn. I know of no other country so versatile in flour varieties. There are corn and cassava cakes in profusion – baked in the oven, directly over the coals or wrapped in corn husks or banana leaves. There are also the beijus, similar to pancakes and made on skillets or hot griddles. But the dry flour, used in many specialities, needs to be combined with other predominantly wet foods to become more enjoyable. That is why they are always associated with Brazil's other great culinary inventions: the moquecas. These stews are so versatile that they almost run the length of the entire Brazilian coast, with local variations. Setting out from the Amazon region, where they are made with freshwater fish and local seasonings, they soon advance along the coast, where coconut milk is added to the dish over more than 7,240 kilometres of coastline. In Bahia, and only in Bahia, they add an African element to the coconut: dendê oil. Following the coast almost as far down as Rio de Janeiro, the dendê disappears. A little further on, so too does the coconut milk, and moqueca becomes a fish stew closer to the European model.

At the opposite extreme, in the backlands of Brazil, the flour varieties win out over the liquid texture of the moquecas. The meat, dried under the sun, salt-preserved or simply cooked or braised until its juices run dry is pounded in a mortar and reduced to small fragments that are mixed with large quantities of cassava flour. These are the paçocas and the cuscuzes. The latter developed only in

São Paulo, from where the pioneers would set off to explore the forests, taking some corn cuscuz in their haversacks for lunch, made like the couscous that the Arabs had learned to eat in the Maghreb.

In the major urban centres, and especially in Salvador and Rio de Janeiro, other dishes have evolved as the result of a compromise between dry and soup-like foodstuffs, such as porridges, pirões and farofas – and the wider use of beans. These are the typical foods of the Bahian Recôncavo Bay region, derived from the religious cults of Candomblé: porridges and pirões made with cassava, corn or rice flour.

But what about feijoada? Feijoada is everywhere, because beans are as important as flour in the Brazilian diet – a bean stew found in all Brazilian homes and to which you can add pieces of meat, smoked or unsmoked. Feijoada is accompanied by couve (a type of kale), oranges and white rice. And you sprinkle a spoonful of the indispensable cassava flour on top! Something the whole nation agrees on.

Brazilian cuisine has become a mosaic of flavours and cooking methods, the expression of a new synthesis that is finding its own identity. It has begun to interact with other external influences, brought to the country by European and Asian immigrants who were attracted by the opportunities offered by growing industrialization.

The chefs who present their work in this book are just a small sample of the vigorous on-going movement that gathered momentum with the emergence of nouvelle cuisine, in dialogue with other cuisines. At the same time, these professionals are taking stock of their national culinary past, aided by new techniques and a new aesthetic. Above all, a new Brazilian taste has discovered the pleasure of moving between the past of the native Indians, Africans and Portuguese immigrants, and other more recent arrivals, without fear of losing its identity.

Carlos Alberto Dória, Brazilian sociologist, anthropologist and food writer

O que é a comida brasileira? } What is Brazilian food?

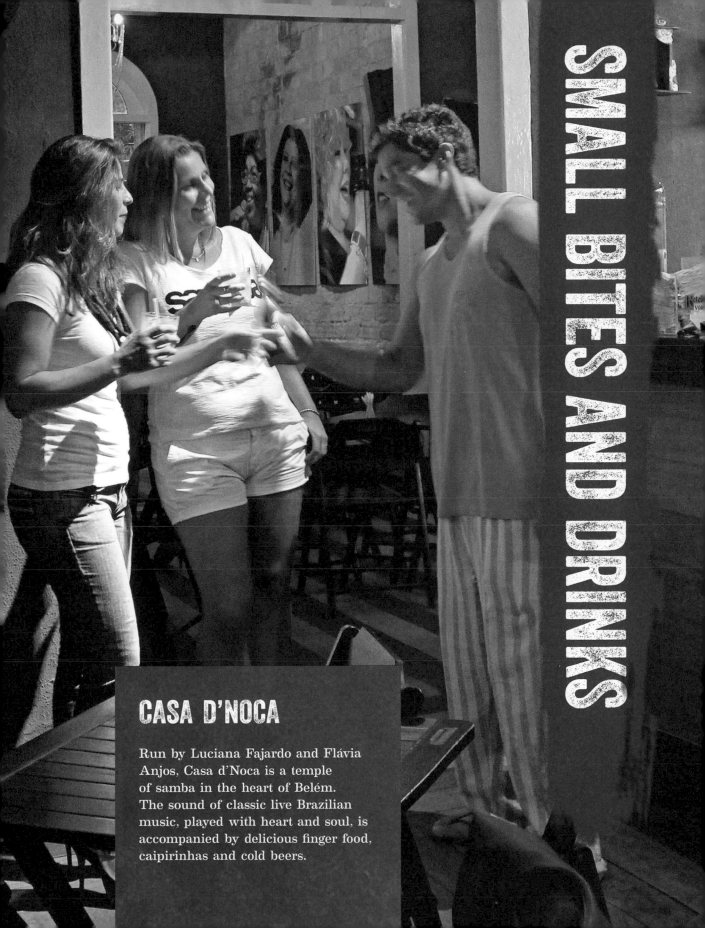

CASA D'NOCA

Run by Luciana Fajardo and Flávia Anjos, Casa d'Noca is a temple of samba in the heart of Belém. The sound of classic live Brazilian music, played with heart and soul, is accompanied by delicious finger food, caipirinhas and cold beers.

Bolinho de piracuí
Fish balls

This appetizer is a classic dish of Santarém, one of the oldest cities in the Amazon. Known as the Pearl of the Tapajós, Santarém is situated between the Tapajós and Amazon rivers, where the spectacular meeting of these waters is a popular tourist attraction. My father, who lived there for many years, taught me this recipe, which is prepared with piracuí – a type of fishmeal or fish flour typical of the region.

Makes 20 balls

* 300g potatoes, peeled
* 30ml extra virgin olive oil
* 50g onion, finely chopped
* 50g tomatoes, diced
* 10g garlic, crushed
* 1 pimenta-de-cheiro or other mild chilli
* 430g piracuí or pre-soaked salt cod (see tip, below)
* 240g plain flour
* 80g queijo do Marajó or creamy Lancashire cheese, grated
* 1 tbsp chopped culantro (Mexican/long coriander)
* 1 tbsp chopped basil
* 1 egg, beaten, plus 3 eggs extra, beaten
* salt
* corn oil, for deep-frying
* 200g panko Japanese breadcrumbs

Tips from Thiago:
To prepare the salt cod for this recipe, soak it in cold water for 48 hours, changing the water every 12 hours. Then discard the bones and skin and grind it in a food processor, or finely chop before use.

1. Cook the potatoes in a saucepan of boiling water until they are fork tender. Drain and let cool, then mash and set aside.

2. Heat the olive oil in a frying pan and sauté the onion, tomato, garlic and pimenta-de-cheiro until softened.

3. Add 400g of the piracuí and sauté for a few more seconds. Add the mashed potato, 40g of the flour, the cheese and fresh herbs and stir well to combine. Remove from the heat and let the mixture cool slightly.

4. Add 1 beaten egg and stir well. Adjust the salt to taste and leave to cool completely.

5. Shape the mixture into golf-ball-sized balls, or the size you want.

6. In a deep-fat fryer or heavy-based saucepan, preheat the corn oil to 170°C. Prepare three shallow bowls: one containing the remaining 200g of flour, one with the remaining 3 beaten eggs and one with the panko mixed with the last 30g of the piracuí.

7. Dip the balls first in the flour, then in the eggs and finally in the breadcrumb and piracuí mixture, turning to ensure they are well coated.

8. Deep-fry the balls, a few at a time, until golden brown, then remove with a slotted spoon and drain on kitchen paper. Serve hot.

Camarão empanado no aviú
Aviú-breaded shrimps

Aviú are micro-shrimp, about 8mm long, and are abundant on the surface of Amazonian rivers after the first floods and found mainly on the river Tapajós. A recipe such as this would usually be made with breadcrumbs, but I found the idea of coating shrimp (prawns) with shrimp very playful!

Serves 2

* 150g raw peeled prawns, with tails
* salt and black pepper
* vegetable oil, for deep-frying
* 70g plain flour
* 2 eggs, beaten
* 30g aviú (tiny dried, salty shrimp) or finely chopped regular dried salt shrimps

1. Season the prawns with salt and black pepper.

2. In a deep-fat fryer or heavy-based saucepan, preheat the oil to 170°C. Meanwhile, prepare three shallow bowls: one containing the flour, one with the beaten eggs and one for the aviú. Dip the prawns first in the flour, then in the eggs, and finally in the aviú, turning to ensure they are well coated.

3. Deep-fry the prawns, in batches, until golden brown, then remove with a slotted spoon and drain on kitchen paper.

Tips from Thiago:
Serve with lime wedges and Pepper Jelly (see page 102), or any hot pepper sauce.

Torresmo de peixe com molho de açaí

Fish crackling with açai

One of Pará's traditional street foods is Fried Fish with Açai (see page 50). Every morning when I go shopping at Ver-o-Peso market, I stop at Léo's tent to drink an açai, which is served with farinha d' água and crispy-skinned fried fish. This recipe was inspired by that Paraense ritual – at the restaurant we created a snack using the skin of the fish that a lot of people at home would often rather discard.

Serves 4

Fish crackling

* 500g fish skin, from small lean fish (see tips, below)
* 150g coarse rock salt
* vegetable oil, for deep-frying
* sea salt flakes

Açai juice

* 100g açai pulp
* juice of 1 lime
* 2 tbsp sugar
* salt, to taste

1. Clean the fish skin, removing the scales. Prepare a brining solution with the rock salt and 500ml of water in a bowl. Soak the fish skins in this liquid for 20 minutes.

2. To make the juice, mix the açai, lime juice and sugar together with a pinch of salt.

3. Bring some water to the boil in a saucepan. Remove the fish skins from the brine and scald them briefly in the boiling water. Drain and cool.

4. Using a sharp knife, remove any remaining flesh from the skins. Cut the skins into 10cm squares.

5. In a deep-fat fryer or heavy-based saucepan, preheat the oil to 180°C. Use kitchen paper to thoroughly pat dry the squares of fish skin. Working in batches, deep-fry the skin squares until they crackle.

6. Remove with a slotted spoon and drain on kitchen paper. Sprinkle with sea salt before serving with the açai juice.

Tips from Thiago:
Use the skin of small fish for this recipe, as it is thinner. If you only have thicker fish skin available, you will need to dehydrate the squares before frying them: follow the recipe as above and after cutting the fish skins into squares, place them in a dehydrator at 65°C for $1\frac{1}{2}$ hours. Alternatively, place on a baking sheet and bake in the oven at 65°C (150°F), gas mark <$\frac{1}{4}$ for the same time.

Isca de peixe empanada na farinha de tapioca

Tapioca fish bites

This snack is a Brazilian favourite. Fish bites, accompanied by a caipirinha or cold beer, are served in pubs, as street food and even at home, as an appetizer. There are several ways of coating the fish – for example, using breadcrumbs, shredded coconut or beer batter. The fish bites we serve at our restaurant are rolled in farinha de tapioca (puffed tapioca flakes from Pará) that look like tapioca pearls, but are as lightweight and crispy as puffed rice.

Serves 2

* 200g skinless pirarucu (arapaima) fillets, or cod
* salt and black pepper
* 80g plain flour
* 3 eggs, beaten
* 80g farinha de tapioca (for a substitute, see page 82) or granulated tapioca
* vegetable oil, for deep-frying

1. Cut the fish into strips 1cm thick and 3cm long. Season with salt and pepper. In a deep-fat fryer or heavy-based saucepan, preheat the oil to 180°C.

2. Prepare three shallow bowls: one containing the flour, one with the beaten eggs and one with the tapioca. Dip the fish strips first in the flour, then in the eggs, and finally in the tapioca, turning to ensure they are well coated.

3. Deep-fry the fish bites, in batches, until light golden brown, then remove with a slotted spoon and drain on kitchen paper. Serve hot.

Tips from Thiago:
Serve the fish bites accompanied by Pickled Cumari-do-Pará Chillies (see page 102) or lime wedges.

Janaina Rueda opened Bar da Dona Onça (Bar of Mrs Leopard) in 2008 in São Paulo with the aim of rescuing bar food from the 1950s and promoting traditional rural dishes. Comfort food is at the top of her agenda. Bar da Dona Onça's finger food is irresistible and the cocktails are made with artisan cachaças.

Janaina's husband, Jefferson Rueda, is the chef of Attimo, the latest hot restaurant in Brazil, but in earlier years the couple worked together, turning Bar da Dona Onça into one of the most beloved addresses for casual food in São Paulo. The Bar is proud to have won prizes for the best feijoada, and best bar in the city. It is one of the most authentic places for Brazilian cuisine in the country, and when you meet Janaina and Jefferson Rueda you will know why...

Coxinha de galinha caipira
Teardrop-shaped chicken croquettes

This is the most beloved salgadinho or bar snack in São Paulo state, and one of the most famous from Brazil. Whether in bars or at parties, these coxinhas are served in all sizes: small ones for appetizers, others almost as large as a pear. This recipe is served at the Bar da Dona Onça. It's impossible to eat just one.

Makes 40

* 1kg free-range chicken legs
* salt and black pepper
* 17g garlic, crushed
* ½ tsp dried thyme leaves
* ½ tsp dried rosemary leaves
* vegetable oil, for deep- and shallow-frying
* ½ carrot, diced
* 1 onion, cubed, plus ½ onion, finely chopped
* ½ celery stalk
* 15g arrowroot
* 65g butter
* 15ml annatto (achiote) oil
* 450g plain flour
* 1–2 eggs
* 200g fine breadcrumbs

* You will also need a pressure cooker

1. Season the chicken with 15g of salt, some black pepper, 10g of the garlic, the thyme and rosemary. Refrigerate for 12 hours.

2. Heat a drizzle of vegetable oil in a pressure cooker and brown the chicken legs on all sides. Add the carrot, the cubed onion and the celery, and pour in enough cold water to cover. Pressure cook for about 20 minutes.

3. Remove the chicken from the stock and leave to cool slightly. Reserve 500ml of the stock. Pull the meat from the bones and shred it.

4. Melt 15g of the butter in a clean saucepan and brown the finely chopped onion. Add the remaining crushed garlic and the annatto oil.

5. Dissolve the arrowroot in 250ml of the reserved chicken stock and stir it into the pan along with the chicken. Cook over a low heat for about 20 minutes, stirring occasionally. Set aside.

6. Heat the remaining 250ml of chicken stock in a medium saucepan with 50g of butter. When it comes to the boil, lower the heat and add 250g of the flour to the pan all at once. Cook, stirring constantly, until the dough forms a ball that pulls away from the sides of the pan. Leave until cool enough to handle.

7. Take a piece of dough and press it into a 5mm-deep disc in the palm of your hand. Place some of the chicken mixture in the centre – if you are making small coxinhas (the size of a ping-pong ball), you will need about 2 teaspoons of filling. Mould the dough around the filling with your fingertips to form a pear shape.

8. Prepare three bowls for the coating: one containing the remaining 200g of flour, one with the beaten eggs and one with the breadcrumbs. Dip the coxinhas first in the flour, then in the eggs and finally in the breadcrumbs, turning to ensure they are well coated.

9. Refrigerate for a few hours to set, but remove from the fridge before frying to allow them to return to room temperature.

10. In a deep-fat fryer or heavy-based saucepan preheat the vegetable oil to 170°C. Deep-fry the coxinhas, a few at a time, until golden brown. Remove with a slotted spoon and drain on kitchen paper. Serve hot.

Tips from Janaina and Jefferson:
A drop of hot red pepper sauce, such as Tabasco, makes the coxinhas even more delicious. You can freeze any leftovers and reheat them in the oven.

Croquete de bochecha de boi
Beef cheek croquettes

Salgadinhos – savoury bite-sized snacks – are a Brazilian tradition served in pubs, kiosks by the beach and at family parties. This croquette recipe uses beef cheeks, a delicious cut of meat that is often overlooked.

Makes 40

* 1kg beef cheeks, trimmed
* 20g salt
* 3 garlic cloves, crushed
* ½ tsp thyme leaves
* ½ tsp chopped rosemary
* vegetable oil, for deep- and shallow-frying
* 50g butter
* 1 onion, finely chopped
* 40g arrowroot
* 200g cooked mashed potatoes
* pinch of black pepper
* 50g mixture chopped flat-leaf parsley and spring onions
* 1 egg yolk, plus 3 eggs, lightly beaten
* 250g plain flour
* 250g fine dried breadcrumbs

* You will also need a pressure cooker

1. Season the meat with the salt, garlic, thyme and rosemary and marinate in the refrigerator for 12 hours.

2. Heat 2 tablespoons of vegetable oil in a pressure cooker and brown the meat on all sides. Add enough cold water to cover. Pressure cook for about 50 minutes.

3. Remove the meat from the pressure cooker and set the broth aside until cool. Grind the meat using a meat grinder, or pulse it in a food processor.

4. Melt the butter in a large saucepan and sauté the onion until golden brown. Add the ground cooked beef and sauté for 3 minutes.

5. Dissolve the arrowroot in the cooled cooking broth, then add it to the meat and cook, stirring constantly, until the mixture pulls away from the sides of the pan. Remove from the heat and leave to cool.

6. Stir the mashed potato, black pepper, chopped parsley and spring onions into the meat mixture. Taste and adjust the salt as needed. Add the egg yolk and stir well to combine.

7. Shape the mixture into balls the size of a golf ball, then, if desired, elongate them to give a traditional log shape to the croquettes.

8. In a deep-fat fryer or heavy-based saucepan, heat the oil to 170°C. Prepare three shallow bowls: one containing the flour, one with the beaten eggs and one with the breadcrumbs. Dip the croquettes first in the flour, then in the eggs and finally in the breadcrumbs, turning to ensure they are well coated.

9. Deep-fry the croquettes, a few at a time, until they are golden and crisp on the outside. Remove with a slotted spoon and place on kitchen paper to drain before serving.

Tips from Janaina and Jefferson:
If you don't have a pressure cooker, use a heavy-based pan or casserole and cook the beef cheeks over a medium-low heat for about 1½ hours, until the meat starts to fall apart.

Bolinho de pirarucu empanado na farinha-d'água
Fish croquettes

The pirarucu, a fish native to the Amazon region, is one of the largest freshwater fish in the world. It can reach 3 metres in length, weigh 250 kilograms, and yet it has barely any bones. Pirarucu is sold fresh, salted or dried – you need the salted variety for this recipe. People also call it the Amazonian cod or Amazonian salted cod.

Makes 30

* 600g salted pirarucu (arapaima) or salt cod fillets
* 100g onion, cut into large cubes, plus 50g finely diced onion
* 300g even-sized whole potatoes, peeled
* 30ml olive oil
* 30g butter
* 1 tbsp chopped garlic
* 50g tomato, chopped
* 2 tbsp chopped pimenta-de-cheiro or other mild chilli
* 2 tbsp hand-torn culantro (Mexican/long coriander)
* 2 tbsp chopped basil
* 240g plain flour
* 50g queijo do Marajó or creamy Lancashire cheese, grated
* 5 eggs
* corn oil, for deep-frying
* 200g fine farinha-d'água or fine breadcrumbs

Tips from Thiago:
These croquettes are best served with Coconut Milk Sauce (see page 103).

1. Soak the salted pirarucu in plenty of cold water for 12 hours, changing the water every 3 hours.

2. Put 2 litres of fresh water in a saucepan with the cubes of onion and bring to the boil. Add the drained pirarucu and cook for 8 minutes or until tender. Lift the fish from the water, flake it and set aside.

3. In the same pan of water, boil the potatoes until tender but still firm. Drain, then mash and set aside.

4. Heat the olive oil and butter in a separate large saucepan. Add the garlic, finely diced onion, tomato, chilli, culantro and basil and sauté until wilted. Stir in the flaked fish and sauté for a few more minutes.

5. Add the mashed potato, 40g of the flour and the cheese and continue cooking for 4 minutes, stirring constantly, until the mixture forms a ball that pulls away from the sides of the pan.

6. Remove from the heat and set aside until cool enough to handle. Add 1 egg and stir to combine. Leave to cool completely, then refrigerate for 30 minutes to set the mixture and make it easier to roll the croquettes.

7. Using a tablespoon as a measuring guide, shape the mixture into logs. In a deep-fat fryer or heavy-based saucepan, preheat the corn oil to 170°C.

8. Prepare three shallow bowls for the coating: one containing the remaining 200g of flour, one with the remaining 4 eggs, beaten, and one with the farinha-d'água. Dip the croquettes first in the flour, then in the eggs, and finally in the farinha d'água, turning to ensure they are well coated.

9. Deep-fry the croquettes a few at a time until golden brown. Remove with a slotted spoon and place on kitchen paper to drain. Serve hot.

Rodrigo Oliveira

Dadinhos de tapioca com queijo coalho e molho de pimenta agridoce

Fried cheese cubes with sweet chilli sauce

This classic recipe is from the acclaimed restaurant Mocotó run by Rodrigo Oliveira (see page 174). The golden, crispy-skinned cubes packed with melted cheese, combined with the sweet and sour flavour of the chilli sauce, are a perfect combination with caipirinhas (see page 38).

Serves 8

* 500ml whole milk
* 250g queijo de coalho or halloumi cheese, grated
* 250g granulated tapioca
* about 8g salt
* pinch of white pepper
* vegetable oil, for deep-frying
* Chilli Sauce, to serve (see right)

1. Gently heat the milk to scalding point in a small saucepan.

2. Combine the cheese and tapioca in a bowl. Slowly add the hot milk, stirring constantly to prevent lumps forming.

3. Add the salt (you may need more or less depending on the saltiness of the cheese) and pepper and continue stirring until the mixture thickens.

4. Line a baking tin with cling film and pour the cheese mixture into it. Cover the surface with more cling film to prevent a skin forming. Leave to cool, then refrigerate for at least 4 hours.

5. Preheat the oil to 180°C in a deep-fat fryer or heavy-based saucepan. Take the cheese mixture out of the tin and cut into cubes. Deep-fry in small batches until golden brown. Alternatively bake the cubes in a preheated oven at 190°C (375°F), gas mark 5.

6. Serve hot with chilli sauce.

Sweet chilli sauce Makes 1 litre

* 17g garlic cloves, left whole
* 8g pimenta dedo-de-moça, or other hot red chillies, left whole
* 60g kiss peppers or other sweet mild chillies
* 30g bird's-eye chillies
* 190ml mango vinegar
* 375g sugar
* 15g salt
* 30ml white cachaça
* 17g polvilho doce (sweet cassava starch)

1. Preheat the oven to 150°C (300°F), gas mark 2. Put the garlic cloves and chillies in their skins on a baking sheet and bake for 18 minutes, then peel.

2. Transfer the cooked garlic and chillies to a food processor or blender. Add half the kiss peppers and pulse to a coarse paste. Place in a bowl and set aside.

3. In the same processor (no need to wash it up), finely chop the bird's-eye chillies with the remaining kiss peppers. Discard any excess liquid that forms and add this mixture to the garlic and chilli paste.

4. Combine the vinegar, half the sugar, the salt and cachaça in a medium saucepan. Place over a low heat and stir constantly until the mixture comes to the boil. Turn off the heat and keep warm.

5. In a large heavy-based saucepan, slowly dissolve the remaining sugar until a golden brown caramel forms. Very carefully add 50ml of water and stir until smooth. Add the chilli and garlic paste and stir well to combine.

6. Reheat the vinegar mixture to bring it to a rolling boil. Gradually pour it into the chilli caramel, being careful not to burn yourself by hot spills.

7. Dissolve the polvilho doce in 200ml of water and stir well to combine. Add it to the chilli sauce, stirring constantly.

8. Increase the heat and simmer, stirring constantly, until the mixture reaches gelling point. Leave to cool, then place in a sterilized airtight bottle or jar. Store in the refrigerator and use within 1 week.

Tips from Rodrigo:

If you don't want to make your own chilli sauce, try serving these cheesy cubes with a shop-bought sweet chilli dipping sauce.

Patas de caranguejo no coco
Coconut crab claws

This delicious appetizer is quick to make. The coating works well for prawns too.

Serves 2

* 140g peeled crab claws
* salt and black pepper
* coconut oil or vegetable oil, for deep-frying
* 50g plain flour
* 2 eggs, beaten
* 50g unsweetened, finely shredded desiccated coconut

1. Season the crab claws with salt and black pepper.

2. In a deep-fat fryer or heavy-based saucepan, preheat the oil to 180°C. Prepare three shallow bowls for the coating: one containing the flour, one with the beaten eggs and one with the desiccated coconut.

3. Dip the crab claws first in the flour, then in the eggs and finally in the coconut, turning to make sure that the claws are completely coated.

4. Deep-fry the crab claws until they are golden brown, then remove with a slotted spoon and drain on kitchen paper before serving.

Tips from Thiago:
Serve with Pepper Jelly (see page 102)
and lime wedges.

LEANDRO BATISTA

Leandro, the cachaça sommelier of Mocotó bar in São Paulo is one of the most knowledgeable people in Brazil on the subject of cachaça. He has created a very special list at Mocotó, with 150 cachaça labels, prioritizing small artisans who make rare or unique spirits.

The bar has become a point of reference for cachaça- and caipirinha-lovers in Brazil. Leandro is constantly travelling around the country to discover new treasures and also organizes tastings and courses. He believes that, one day, cachaça will be the number one drink in the world!

WHAT IS CACHAÇA?

by Leandro Batista, cachaça master at Mocotó bar

Cachaça is an alcoholic beverage made in Brazil and distilled from local sugarcane – in other words, an all-Brazilian speciality. First recorded at a sugar mill in the captaincy of São Vicente circa 1532, the story of cachaça is fascinating and intertwined with the history of colonization, when it served as 'fuel' for the explorers of the new land. As time passed, cachaça evolved, and nowadays our caninha or 'little sugarcane' (another of the hundreds of names cachaça has in Brazil) is one of the world's most consumed spirits, enthralling more and more people.

HOW GOOD-QUALITY CACHAÇA IS PRODUCED

Harvest
The sugarcane should be harvested at its peak of ripeness and sweetness. It should also be pressed as soon as possible, and the sugarcane juice (garapa) transferred to fermentation vats.

Fermentation
One of the most important steps of production. During fermentation yeast converts the sugar in the garapa to alcohol, producing the so-called mosto or 'sugarcane wine'.

Distillation
The mosto is heated in copper stills and the alcohol begins to evaporate. When the steam condenses, we have cachaça. The first portion that starts to drip from the still is called the 'head' – it is not used to make the beverage, and neither is the final part, the 'tail'. Only the 'heart' is converted into cachaça.

Ageing
Once distilled, cachaça is left to age in barrels made of amburana, jequitibá, ipê, balm, amendoim and oak, among others woods.

TO ENJOY YOUR CACHAÇA

* Use a clear, colourless glass or goblet. Look at the cachaça and check that it is limpid and free of sediment.

* Swirl the liquid inside the glass a few times and check its viscosity. The cachaça must leave streaks in the inner walls of the glass, known as choro (literally, 'crying').

* Swirl the cachaça again and gently inhale its aroma.

* Take a first sip, swirling the cachaça in your mouth. Keep it on top of your tongue for a few moments and notice where it is most strongly sensed.

* Swallow the cachaça, observing the path it travels and analysing the satisfaction the spirit provides.

* A taste of cachaça is genuinely a taste of Brazil – cheers!

Cashew fruit caipirinha

* 1 cashew fruit, peeled and cubed
* 2 tbsp caster sugar
* 4–8 ice cubes, crushed if you prefer
* 60ml cachaça

Put the cashew fruit and sugar in a cocktail shaker and crush with a pestle. Add the ice and cachaça and mix well to combine.

Serve in a small, clear glass tumbler.

Classic caipirinha

* 1 lime, sliced
* 2 tbsp caster sugar
* 4–8 ice cubes, crushed if you prefer
* 60ml cachaça

Put the lime and sugar in a big glass or cocktail shaker and crush with a pestle. Add the ice and cachaça and mix well to combine.

Serve in a small, clear glass tumbler.

Jaboticaba caipirinha

* 15 jaboticabas
* 2 tbsp caster sugar
* 4–8 ice cubes, crushed if you prefer
* 60ml cachaça

Put the jaboticabas and sugar in a cocktail shaker and crush with a pestle. Add the ice and cachaça and shake well to combine.

Serve in a small, clear glass tumbler.

Tips from Leandro:
Be creative when preparing your caipirinhas and try using other fresh fruits. Tangerine, lime and lemon; orange and ginger; and passion fruit caipirinhas, for example, are all popular in Brazil.

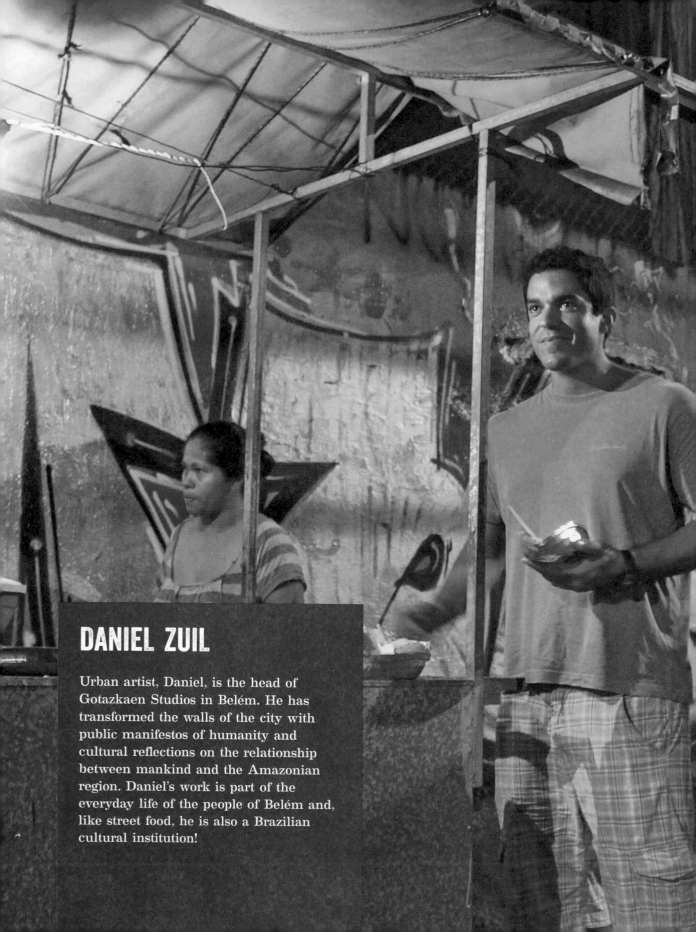

DANIEL ZUIL

Urban artist, Daniel, is the head of Gotazkaen Studios in Belém. He has transformed the walls of the city with public manifestos of humanity and cultural reflections on the relationship between mankind and the Amazonian region. Daniel's work is part of the everyday life of the people of Belém and, like street food, he is also a Brazilian cultural institution!

STREET FOOD

Bolo de macaxeira da dona Carmem
Mrs. Carmem's Cassava Cake

Living in a house with three professional cooks, my mum, Mrs Carmem, does not have much opportunity to cook. We almost always eat at one of our restaurants, both for lunch and for dinner. However, on weekends she spoils the family with her delicious cassava cake – the best in the world for us!

Serves 12

* 2 tbsp butter, for greasing
* 1kg raw cassava, peeled and coarsely grated
* 400ml unsweetened coconut milk
* 160g caster sugar
* 1 tsp salt
* 5 large free-range eggs
* 1 tbsp fennel seeds
* 200g unsweetened, finely shredded desiccated coconut

1. Preheat the oven to 180°C (350°F), gas mark 4, and use the butter to grease a 25 x 30cm rectangular cake tin.

2. Combine the grated cassava, coconut milk, sugar, salt, eggs, fennel seeds and desiccated coconut in a mixing bowl and stir until a smooth batter forms.

3. Pour the mixture into the prepared tin and bake for 40 minutes or until the top is golden brown. Remove from the oven and serve warm.

Tips from Thiago:
This cake is a perfect accompaniment to a freshly ground and brewed Brazilian coffee. Our cafezinho is served in demitasses. It is not as strong as an espresso, but neither is it as diluted as an americano.

Vatapá da Maria Helena

Maria Helena's shrimp and coconut creamy stew

Vatapá is a part of daily life in Belém. Of African origin, it first became famous in Brazil as a traditional dish of Bahia state, though its popularity has since spread throughout the country. You can now find it sold on the streets of several Brazilian states. Some recipes use wheat flour as a thickener, but this one uses bread, which gives this recipe a much more delicate texture. This version of the traditional recipe from Pará is by Maria Helena, one of our cooks at the Remanso do Bosque restaurant.

Serves 10

* 700g dried salt shrimps
* 300g day-old baguette
* 200ml unsweetened coconut milk
* 40ml extra virgin olive oil
* 50g onion, chopped
* 1 garlic clove, crushed
* 35g tomato, diced
* 2 pimentas-de-cheiro or other mild chillies, deseeded and chopped
* 2 bay leaves
* ¼ tsp ground cumin
* ¾ tsp colorau or ground annatto (achiote)
* 10ml dendê (palm) oil
* salt and black pepper
* 5g culantro (Mexican/ long coriander) or coriander leaves, torn into pieces
* 5g basil leaves, torn into pieces

To serve
* 50g dried salt shrimps, heads removed
* 150g jambu (Pará cress/ toothache plant) or watercress or spinach leaves
* Brazilian-style White Rice (see page 94)

1. Soak the whole dried shrimps in plenty of cold water for 4 hours. Drain and peel, reserving the shrimp heads and shells. Put the shrimp in a colander and rinse well under cold running water.

2. Put the shrimp heads and shells in a blender with 1 litre of fresh water and process until smooth. Transfer the liquid to a large saucepan and boil for 10 minutes until you have a flavourful shrimp broth. Remove from the heat, strain the mixture through a sieve and set aside.

3. Tear the baguette into small pieces and put them in a bowl. Add the coconut milk and 150ml of water and leave to soak for 20 minutes.

4. Heat the olive oil in a large saucepan. Add the onion, garlic, tomato and chillies and sauté until softened.

5. Stir in the peeled shrimps and sauté for 1 minute. Stir in the shrimp broth and heat until the mixture reaches simmering point. Add the bay leaves.

6. Gradually add the soaked bread mixture to the pan, stirring constantly, and cook for 5 minutes or until thickened. If necessary, add more soaked bread or let the sauce reduce a little until it reaches a sauce-like consistency.

7. Add the ground cumin, colorau, dendê oil and some black pepper. Reduce the heat and leave to cook for 4 minutes.

8. Stir in the fresh herbs. Season to taste with salt – don't add too much as this will mask the sweetness of the sauce.

9. Prepare the garnishes. Using a colander, rinse the additional dried shrimps under cold running water to remove excess salt. Cook them in a large saucepan of boiling water for 4 minutes, then remove with a slotted spoon and set aside.

10. Rinse the jambu leaves and plunge them into the boiling water for 1 minute. Drain then plunge them immediately into a bowl of iced water to stop the cooking and keep their bright green colour. Serve the vatapá with Brazilian-style White Rice and the prepared garnishes.

Tips from Thiago:
Dried salt shrimps are available from African and Asian food shops. You can prepare your own using large fresh raw shrimps by covering them in salt and leaving them in the refrigerator overnight. Alternatively, you can substitute them with salt cod, cooked fish or chicken, in which case prepare the broth with your chosen ingredient.

Maniçoba com costela de porco
Cassava leaf and pork stew served with pork ribs

One of the most emblematic dishes of the Brazilian Amazon, maniçoba is also known as 'Amazonian feijoada'. Together with Duck in Cassava Juice Sauce (see page 186), it symbolizes the Pará feast prepared for the great Círio de Nazaré religious festival. This takes place in Belém in October and attracts more than one million people to the city.

Serves 15

* 300g forequarter charque, cut into cubes
* 1 salted pig's ear, roughly chopped
* 1 salted pig's trotter, cut into 3 pieces
* 2kg ready-cooked cassava leaves
* 300g slab bacon, cut into 2cm cubes
* 300g bone-in smoked pork ribs, separated
* 400g bone-in pork neck, cut into 4cm pieces
* 4 bay leaves
* 40ml extra virgin olive oil
* 50g onion, finely diced
* 10g garlic, crushed
* 3 tbsp coarsely chopped culantro (Mexican/long coriander)
* 2 tbsp chopped coriander sprigs

* 2 cumari-do-Pará or other mild yellow chillies, deseeded and chopped
* ½ tbsp ground cumin
* ½ tbsp freshly ground black pepper

Salt pork ribs
* 1.5kg rack of pork ribs
* 1 tbsp chopped garlic
* 1 tbsp brown sugar
* 1 tbsp salt
* black pepper
* 1 tsp fennel seeds
* juice of ½ lime

1. Put the charque, pig's ear and trotter in a large bowl. Cover with cold water and soak for 12 hours, changing the water every 4 hours to remove the excess salt.

2. Combine the precooked cassava leaves with 3 litres of water in a large, heavy-based pot. Cook over a medium heat for 12 hours, adding more water as needed to prevent it boiling dry.

3. Add the bacon and charque to the pot and cook over a low heat for a further 2 hours.

4. Add the pig's ear and trotter, smoked pork ribs, pork neck and bay leaves to the pot. Continue cooking for a further 2 hours over a low heat.

5. Heat the olive oil in a frying pan and sauté the onion, garlic, culantro, coriander, cumari-do-Pará, cumin and black pepper. Add this to the pot of maniçoba and cook for 30 minutes. Taste and add salt if necessary.

6. To prepare the pork ribs, mix together the garlic, brown sugar, salt and pepper, fennel seeds and lime juice. Rub this mixture over the ribs and leave to marinate in the refrigerator for 1 hour. Preheat the oven to 180°C (350°F), gas mark 4. Wrap the rack of ribs in aluminium foil and bake for 1 hour.

7. Preheat a charcoal barbecue. Remove the ribs from the oven and discard the foil. Sit the ribs 40cm above the hot coals and chargrill for 5 minutes on each side or until golden brown. Cut the ribs into sections and serve with the maniçoba.

Tips from Thiago:

Cassava leaves are always sold either cooked or frozen and can be found in African food shops. You will find salted pork and beef in Brazilian and Portuguese butchers, or sold as a kit for feijoada, in Brazilian stores.

Serve with Brazilian-style White Rice (see page 94) and Pickled Cumari-do Pará Chillies (see page 102), as well as fine, untoasted cassava flour to sprinkle over the broth.

Peixe frito com açaí
Fried fish with açai

In Belém, açai is as important as beans or rice, the two basic elements of everyday eating for most Brazilians. These Amazonian berries are not consumed as an energy booster or dessert the way they are usually eaten in other parts of Brazil and abroad, but as an accompaniment for savoury dishes instead. At Ver-o-Peso, Brazil's most famous market, the berries are served puréed, no sugar added, with fried fish and cassava flour.

Serves 3

* 300g pratiqueira, cleaned and gutted, or mullet or trout fillets
* salt and black pepper
* 2 tsp lime juice
* corn oil, for deep-frying
* 100g plain flour
* 3 eggs, lightly beaten
* 100g farinha-d'água, toasted cassava flour or fine breadcrumbs
* açai pulp, to serve (eat all you want!)

1. Season the fish with salt, black pepper and lime juice. Pat dry with kitchen paper. In a deep-fryer or heavy-based saucepan, heat the oil to 170°C.

2. Prepare three shallow bowls for the coating, one containing the flour, one with the beaten eggs and one with the farinha-d'água.

3. Dip the fish first in the flour, then in the eggs and finally in the farinha-d'água, turning to ensure they are well coated.

4. Deep-fry the fish, in batches if using pratiqueira or one at a time if using fillets, until golden brown. Remove from the oil and drain on kitchen paper. Serve hot with a bowlful of unseasoned açai pulp at room temperature.

Tips from Thiago:
You can also fry the fish without breading it. To make it really crispy, keep the scales intact. Pat the fish dry thoroughly and deep-fry at 170°C until crisp.

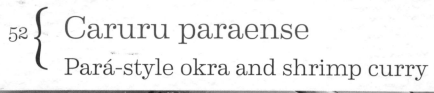

Caruru paraense
Pará-style okra and shrimp curry

The origins of caruru point to a divided authorship between native Indians and Africans. This typical dish of Bahia state is nowadays associated with the African-Brazilian religious ritual, Candomblé, and served as a main course, as here, or as part of a banquet.

Serves 5

* 700g whole dried salt shrimps
* 40ml extra virgin olive oil
* 50g onion, finely chopped
* 1 tbsp crushed garlic
* 15g green pepper, diced
* 35g tomato, chopped
* 2 cumari-do-Pará or other mild yellow chillies, chopped
* 400g okra, cut into 1cm-thick rounds
* 1 bay leaf
* 250g fine, untoasted cassava flour

* pinch of ground cumin
* black pepper
* 20ml dendê (palm) oil
* 1½ tbsp hand-torn culantro (Mexican/long coriander)
* 1½ tbsp hand-torn basil
* 150g jambu (Pará cress/toothache plant) or watercress
* Brazilian-style White Rice (see page 94), to serve
* 50g dried salt shrimps, heads removed

1. Soak the whole dried shrimps in plenty of cold water for 4 hours. Drain and peel, reserving the heads and shells.

2. Put the heads and shells in a colander and rinse well under cold running water. Transfer to a blender, add 1.4 litres of water and process until smooth. Pour the liquid into a large saucepan and bring to the boil over a high heat. Boil hard for 10 minutes to make a full-flavoured broth. Strain and set aside.

3. In a separate saucepan, heat the olive oil and sauté the onion, garlic, green pepper, tomato and cumari-do-Pará until softened.

4. Add the peeled shrimps and okra and sauté for 1 minute. Stir in the shrimp broth and heat until simmering.

5. Add the bay leaf, then gradually add the cassava flour, stirring constantly with a whisk to prevent lumps forming. Cook for 7 minutes or until thickened.

6. Stir in the ground cumin, a little black pepper and the dendê oil. Lower the heat and cook for 4 minutes.

7. Add the culantro and basil, stirring to combine. Adjust the salt to taste and keep the caruru hot while you prepare the garnishes.

8. Rinse the dried shrimps under cold running water to remove excess salt. In a saucepan of boiling water, cook the shrimp for 4 minutes then drain and set aside.

9. Bring another saucepan of water to the boil, add the jambu leaves and blanch them for 1 minute. Drain and refresh in a bowl of iced water to stop the cooking and keep the leaves bright green. Drain before plating.

10. To serve, place a spoonful of cooked white rice on serving plates, add a portion of caruru and garnish with the jambu leaves and shrimps.

Tapioca molhada com leite de castanha

Tapioca crepes with Brazil nut milk

In Mosqueiro, a town next to Belém, the tapioqueiros (tapioca sellers) announce their arrival by shouting through the streets: 'TAPIOQUEEEEEEEEEEIRO!' People are used to being greeted by these voices and their sound is part of daily life. This recipe is one of the most traditional of our region. Usually coconut milk is the ingredient of choice, but in this version we use Brazil nut milk.

Makes 18

* 300g raw Brazil nuts
* 500g goma de mandioca or sweet tapioca starch
* 1 banana leaf (optional)
* salt
* 60g rapadura or dark muscovado sugar
* ¾ tsp fennel seeds

Tips from Thiago:
The tapiocas are better cooked and eaten straight after sifting the starch mixture, as they tend to dry out if sifted in advance.

1. In a saucepan, heat 1 litre of water to 60°C. Carefully pour it into a blender, add the Brazil nuts and process for 3 minutes. Strain the milk into a bowl and reserve the strained nuts (you will need 200g of the ground nuts to finish the recipe).

2. Combine the goma de mandioca and 2 litres of water in a mixing bowl and leave to stand for 1 hour. Carefully drain the water from the bowl, pouring it away slowly to leave the starch behind in the bottom of the bowl. Cover with a clean tea towel and leave it to stand for a further 1 hour, to absorb the excess water.

3. Meanwhile, cut the banana leaf (if using) into 10cm diameter discs. Wave them quickly over an open flame to soften, then set aside.

4. Break the starch into pieces with a spoon, add some salt to taste and pass the mixture through a fine sieve to obtain a fine and fluffy powder.

5. Heat a small nonstick frying pan. Sprinkle some of the starch flour over the base of the pan in a thin, even layer. Cook for 30 seconds, then flip it over and cook for a further 30 seconds. Remove from the heat and set aside while you cook the remainder.

6. Cut out each crepe into circles using a 10cm diameter plain cookie cutter. Moisten each tapioca disc with the Brazil nut milk. Spread a little of the ground Brazil nuts, rapadura and fennel seeds over each of them.

7. Fold each tapioca disc in half and drizzle with some more Brazil nut milk. Wrap in a disc of banana leaf, secure with a cocktail stick and serve.

Tacacá
Cassava, shrimp and Pará cress broth

Many still debate whether the tacacá is a food or a drink. This Brazilian speciality is the symbol of street food in Pará and other Amazonian cities. Drinking tacacá from a gourd bowl in the tents of the tacacazeiras (women who prepare tacacá), is a habit that many people in our region have adopted. It seems contradictory to drink such a hot concoction in a tropical region, but the numbness in the mouth and the heat exchange tacacá provides are a relief, synonymous with comfort.

Serves 10

* 500g peeled dried salt shrimps, with tails
* 300g jambu (Pará cress/toothache plant) or watercress
* 500g goma de mandioca (see tip, below)
* 2 litres Tucupi or Tucupi substitute (see page 104)
* 2 tbsp hand-torn culantro (Mexican/long coriander)
* 2 garlic cloves, crushed
* 2 tbsp hand-torn basil
* 1 tbsp chopped pimenta-de-cheiro or other mild red chilli
* 2 cumari-do-Pará or other mild yellow chillies, deseeded and chopped
* salt

1. Soak the shrimps in plenty of cold water for 4 hours, then drain.

2. Put the shrimps in a saucepan with enough fresh water to cover and place over a high heat. Bring to the boil and cook for 3 minutes. Remove the shrimps from the pan using a slotted spoon and set aside.

3. Add the jambu leaves to the pan and blanch for 2 minutes, then plunge them immediately into a bowl of iced water to stop the cooking. Drain and set aside.

4. In a mixing bowl, combine the goma de mandioca and 300ml of cold water.

5. In a saucepan, bring 400ml of water to the boil. Gradually pour in the goma de mandioca mixture, stirring constantly to prevent lumps. You can use a wire whisk at the beginning, but you will need a spoon once the mixture starts to thicken. Cook for 5 minutes or until clear and thick.

6. In a separate pan, combine the tucupi, culantro, garlic, basil and both types of chilli. Season to taste with salt and cook for 5 minutes.

7. Place a spoonful of the clear, porridge-like mixture and a ladleful of tucupi in each serving bowl and stir to combine. Add a few shrimps and some blanched jambu leaves to each bowl and serve hot.

Tips from Thiago:
If you cannot find goma de mandioca, make the Farinha de Tapioca substitute (see page 82) to the end of step 2.

BETH CHEIROSINHA

'Fragrant Beth' is a specialist in Amazonian herbs and one of the key figures at Ver-o-Peso market. As a small child she absorbed much from her mother and grandmother. Knowledgeable about the medicinal properties of herbs, she is now helping us to learn more about the culinary value of each herb.

VEGETABLES FROM FIELD AND FOREST

Moqueca de banana-da-terra
Plantain and coconut milk stew

Moqueca is a dish of native Indian origin that became famous in Brazil as a traditional preparation of the Bahia state. It is a quite widespread dish, but the states of Espírito Santo and Pará have their own variations. This vegetarian version made with plantain is very easy to prepare.

Serves 4

* 2 whole dried coconuts, to give about 400g shelled, diced coconut meat
* 300g young (green) coconut meat
* 1.5 litres coconut water or tap water, warmed
* 6 black peppercorns
* 1 tsp ground turmeric
* 1 tsp root ginger, finely chopped
* 6 coriander seeds
* 6 cumin seeds
* ½ pimenta dedo-de-moça or other hot red chilli, deseeded
* 60ml dendê (palm) oil
* 40g onion, chopped
* 1 tsp finely chopped garlic
* 30g tomato, chopped
* 1 tsp chopped pimenta-de-cheiro or other mild chilli
* 500g peeled, ripe plantain, cut into thick rounds
* 30g red pepper, cut into large squares
* 1 tbsp coriander leaves
* 1 tsp chopped sweet basil leaves
* juice of ½ lime
* salt

1. Put both types of coconut meat in a blender. Add the warmed coconut water and process for 2 minutes or until smooth. Pass the mixture through a fine sieve and set aside.

2. Combine the black peppercorns, turmeric, ginger, coriander seeds, cumin seeds, chilli pepper and 30ml of the dendê oil in a food processor or mortar. Process or pound together to form a smooth paste.

3. Heat the remaining dendê oil in a medium pot, preferably one made of clay. Add the onion, garlic, tomato, pimenta-de-cheiro and 1 tablespoon of the spice paste. Sauté for a few minutes over a low heat.

4. Add the coconut cream, plantain and red pepper. Cook over a high heat for 5 minutes.

5. Stir in the coriander leaves, basil and lime juice, then season to taste with salt. Cook for a further 2 minutes, then serve.

Tips from Thiago:
This moqueca is ideally served with Coconut Rice (see page 95) or Brazilian-style White Rice (see page 94). Your leftover spice paste can be stored in an airtight container in the refrigerator for up to 10 days. If you can't find young (green) coconut flesh, double the amount of dried coconut used.

Quiabos tostados com pimenta
Chargrilled okra with chilli

Many people hate okra during their childhood because of its slimy texture; however, it deserves to be served regularly at our tables. Besides being delicious, it is packed with vitamins, calcium, fibre and protein. It is highly digestible and low in calories, too (30 kcal per 100g). This recipe can be served either as a main course or an accompaniment.

Serves 6

* 600g okra
* 60ml olive oil
* 4 tbsp aviú (tiny dried, salty shrimp) or chopped regular dried salt shrimps (optional)
* 1 tbsp sea salt flakes
* 2 pimentas dedo-de-moça or other hot red chillies, finely sliced
* 4 tbsp hand-torn coriander leaves
* 2 tbsp lime juice

1. Rinse and pat dry the okra. Place in a bowl and drizzle with the olive oil.

2. Heat a heavy-based cast-iron griddle pan. Add the okra and cook for 3 minutes on each side, being careful not to move them too much, to achieve beautiful grill marks on the exterior.

3. While the okra are still in the pan, season them with the aviú (if using), sea salt, chillies, coriander and lime juice. Remove from the heat and toss well to combine.

Tips from Thiago:

If you want to make this but have difficulty finding aviú or dried shrimps, use katsuobushi (dried smoked tuna), which you can buy in Japanese food stores and some larger supermarkets.

Pupunha com pele de arroz
Peach palm fruit with a rice paper skin

Peach palm fruit are a staple food for the people of Pará and other Amazonian regions. However, when raw they contain peroxidase enzyme, which inhibits the digestion of protein and can cause irritation to the mouth. In order to make them delicious and harmless, the peach palm fruits have to be cooked in boiling water for at least 20 minutes to deactivate this enzyme.

Serves 2

* 250g fresh whole peach palm fruit (see tips, below)
* salt
* 80g butter
* 2 rice paper wrappers
* pinch of ground coffee beans

Tips from Thiago:
Found in Latin food stores, peach palm fruit is also sold brined as pejivalles or chontaduros. If you cannot find them, substitute the fruit with winter squash or pumpkin (such as hokkaido), and the seeds with pumpkin seeds. Preheat the oven to 180°C (350°F), gas mark 4, put the pumpkin seeds in a baking tray and bake for 10 minutes. Remove from the oven, season to taste with salt, then coarsely chop them. Add to the browned butter and proceed as above.

1. Put the peach palm fruit in a saucepan with 60g of salt and enough cold water to cover. Boil for 40-50 minutes or until fork tender.

2. Drain the fruit, peel and cut in half, saving the seeds.

3. Purée the fruit pulp in a blender with 100ml of fresh water. Transfer to a bowl, taste and add salt as necessary, then set aside.

4. Peel and discard the black skin that surrounds the seeds. Chop the white contents on a cutting board and set aside.

5. Heat the butter in a frying pan until it turns golden brown. Add the chopped seeds and coffee, then remove from the heat and set aside.

6. Heat 1 litre of water in a saucepan. Lay the rice paper wrappers side by side in a baking tray. When the water is hot but not boiling, pour it over the rice paper wrappers and leave them to soak for 20 seconds or until malleable.

7. Transfer the wrappers to a clean tea towel to drain.

8. Place a heaped tablespoon of peach palm fruit purée on each serving plate and arrange a rice paper wrapper over the top. Drizzle with a little browned butter and sprinkle with the chopped seeds and ground coffee to serve.

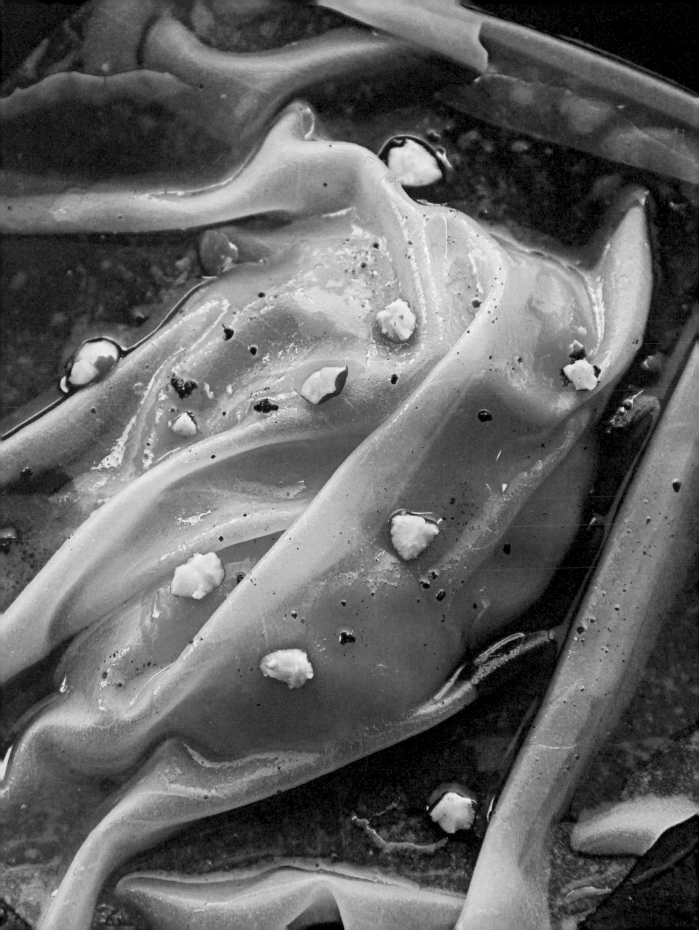

ROBERTA SUDBRACK

Roberta is an autodidact with a very creative mind and was the first woman to be put in charge of the kitchen of a Brazilian president. Her cuisine celebrates Brazilian produce and the best of each season with a modern and elegant approach. Although contemporary, her food has deep roots in tradition. Roberta's Rio de Janeiro restaurant, set in a cosy house in the Botanic Garden area, opened in 2008. Since then, it has become a reference point for Brazilian cuisine.

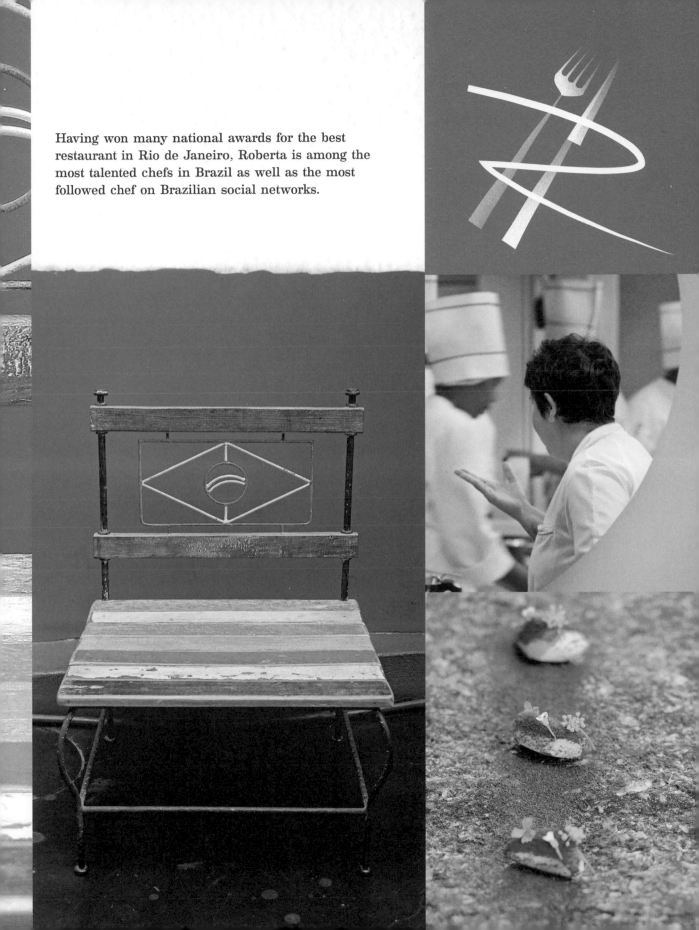

Having won many national awards for the best restaurant in Rio de Janeiro, Roberta is among the most talented chefs in Brazil as well as the most followed chef on Brazilian social networks.

Castanha crua, farinha de banana e brotos

Fresh Brazil nuts, banana flour and assorted sprouts

Brazil nuts, when first harvested, have a texture similar to a freshly opened dry coconut, with white and milky meat. Because they go rancid quickly, they are usually sold already roasted, like those we find in supermarkets. However, at the Ver-o-Peso market in Belém, this oleaginous fruit of Amazonian trees can be purchased fresh. Do try this recipe if you happen to find fresh Brazil nuts.

Makes 8

* 6 ripe lady finger bananas
* caster sugar
* 8 fresh, raw Brazil nuts, peeled, or roasted Brazil nuts
* assorted herb sprouts, microcress and edible flowers, to garnish
* sea salt flakes

1. First make a banana flour. Preheat the oven to 80°C (175°F), gas mark < ¼. Peel the bananas and slice them thinly. Arrange the slices on a silicone mat and sprinkle with a little sugar. Bake for about 3 hours or until the slices are crisp and golden brown. Leave to cool, then grind to a fine powder in a food processor – the texture will be similar to espresso coffee grounds.

2. Pat dry the fresh Brazil nuts and place on a serving plate. Sprinkle with the banana flour, arrange the sprouts and herbs on top and season with sea salt. Serve as an amuse-bouche or starter.

Salada de feijão-manteiguinha com quiabo

Bean and okra salad

The wide variety of beans available in Brazil is one of our greatest gastronomic treasures. Carioca beans (similar to pinto beans) are the most widely consumed in Brazil, followed by black beans. Feijão-manteiguinha, similar in appearance to black-eyed beans, are traditionally used in Santarém, a city in Pará state. This kind of bean does not provide a thick broth, as black beans do. The trick is to serve them al dente.

Serves 5

* 200g dried feijão-manteiguinha or black-eyed beans
* 1 red onion
* 60g caster sugar
* 70ml apple cider vinegar
* 3 coriander seeds
* 100g arracacha (mandioquinha / Peruvian parsnip) or regular parsnip, peeled and cut into 5mm strips, 4cm long
* black pepper
* 10g salt
* 100g okra, cut into 5mm rounds
* 15ml lime juice
* 1 bay leaf
* 1 tbsp coarsely chopped culantro (Mexican/long coriander)
* 3 spring onions, green part only, cut into 2cm lengths
* 1 tbsp flat-leaf parsley
* 1 tbsp coriander leaves
* ½ tbsp finely sliced pimenta-de-cheiro or other mild red chilli
* finely grated zest of ½ lemon
* 40ml extra virgin olive oil

Tips from Thiago:
This salad is usually served as an accompaniment to fatty freshwater fish dishes, such as Chargrilled Fish Ribs (see page 114) and Chargrilled Filhote (see page 110), or with crab claws.

1. Soak the dried beans in plenty of cold water for at least 6 hours.

2. Cut the onion into 6 wedges and pull apart the layers, separating them. Put the onion, sugar, vinegar and coriander seeds in a saucepan and bring to the boil. Turn off the heat, transfer the mixture to a clean glass jar and allow to cool completely. Once cool, seal the jar tightly.

3. Cook the arracacha in a saucepan with 500ml water and the salt for 2 minutes or until al dente (tender but with some bite). Drain and set aside.

4. Combine the okra and lime juice in a bowl and let stand for 10 minutes to help reduce the natural sliminess of the okra. Drain off the lime juice, then cook the okra in a saucepan of boiling water for 3 minutes. Drain and immediately plunge the okra into a bowl of iced water to stop the cooking. Drain and set aside.

5. Drain the beans. Put them in a saucepan with fresh water to cover. Add the bay leaf and simmer for 25 minutes, or until the beans are al dente. Drain in a colander then plunge them into a bowl of iced water. Drain again and transfer to a serving bowl.

6. Add the prepared onions, okra and arracacha to the beans, then add the culantro, spring onions, parsley, coriander leaves, chilli, lemon zest and olive oil. Season to taste with salt and pepper and serve.

Nhoque de banana-da-terra
Plantain gnocchi

The classic Italian gnocchi takes on a tropical character in this recipe, which is a great vegetarian main course or can be served as an accompaniment to fish. Grated Brazil nuts replace the Parmesan cheese.

Serves 6

* 500g ripe plantains, unpeeled
* 1 tbsp ground annatto (achiote)
* salt
* 70g cornflour
* 200g butter
* ½ recipe Banana Leather (see page 236)
* 4 Brazil nuts, grated

Tips from Thiago:
The plantain skins are for decoration only and should not be eaten!

1. Preheat the oven to 180°C (350°F), gas mark 4. Put the unpeeled plantains on a baking sheet and cook for 10 minutes. Make a single cut lengthways into the plantains and scoop out the flesh; you will need to reserve six plantain skins for later. Purée the plantain flesh in a blender or food processor until very smooth. Add the annatto and season to taste with salt.

2. Dissolve the cornflour in 120ml of water.

3. Transfer the puréed plantain to a saucepan and place over a low heat. Gradually add the cornflour mixture to the pan, stirring constantly. Cook for 10 minutes or until the mixture starts to pull away from the sides of the pan. Remove from the heat and allow to cool.

4. Turn the dough onto a clean work surface and shape it into a long rope about 1.5cm wide. Cut into 2cm pieces to make gnocchi. Set aside and keep warm.

5. Melt the butter in a frying pan over a medium-low heat and cook until caramelized – the butter should be golden brown in colour and smell like toasted nuts. Be careful not to overcook it.

6. Preheat the oven to 130°C (260°F), gas mark ½. Place the reserved plantain skins, opened out, on a baking sheet and dry in the oven for 40 minutes.

7. Divide the dried plantain skins among serving plates and place 4 tablespoons of gnocchi in a mound on top. Drizzle with a little brown butter and garnish with pieces of banana leather. Sprinkle with grated Brazil nuts and serve.

Salada de manga verde, chuchu, maxixe e jambo-vermelho

Salad of green mango and rose apple with pickles

Chayote and West Indian gherkin are fruit-vegetables of the same family; cucumber and melon are two of their most distinguished cousins. Their high water contents lend them to salting and pickling. The rose apple, which looks like a Red Anjou pear, also has a high water content. These three, combined with acidic green mango, make a very refreshing salad.

Serves 2

* 280ml apple cider vinegar
* 6 coriander seeds
* 200g caster sugar
* 100g peeled and pitted chayote (cho cho)
* 30g salt
* 100g West Indian gherkin or cucumber
* 200g green mango cheeks, peeled
* 100g rinsed and deseeded jambo-vermelho (rose apple) or hard pear such as Anjou
* 1 tbsp coriander leaves
* 2 tsp beetroot sprouts
* 50ml extra virgin olive oil
* sea salt flakes
* freshly ground white pepper

To serve

* 50g Savoury Cassava Flour Crumble (see page 86)
* 1 tsp finely chopped coriander leaves
* sea salt flakes

1. Combine the vinegar, coriander seeds and sugar in a small saucepan and bring to the boil. Remove from heat and set aside to cool.

2. Slice the chayote very thinly and sprinkle with 15g of the salt. Place in a sieve for 10 minutes, to remove some of the moisture in the vegetable. Rinse the chayote under cold running water, then transfer to a preserving jar and add half the spiced vinegar. Close tightly and refrigerate. The pickles are more flavourful after the second day.

3. Repeat this process with the West Indian gherkin.

4. In a bowl, combine the savoury cassava flour crumble with 30ml water, the chopped coriander and salt to taste and set aside.

5. When almost ready to serve, use a mandolin to slice the green mango and rose apple thinly. Arrange them artistically on a salad plate. Drain the pickled chayote and West Indian gherkin and add them to the dish. Garnish the salad with small spoonfuls of the cassava flour crumble.

6. Scatter the coriander leaves and beetroot sprouts over the salad. Sprinkle with the olive oil, sea salt flakes and white pepper to taste.

Tips from Thiago:
To prevent the chayote's sticky sap staining your hands, peel it under cold running water, cut it in half lengthways, then hold under running water again while you remove the pit.

Batata-doce assada com manteiga de garrafa

Baked sweet potatoes with clarified butter

This is a Brazilian version of baked potatoes. It can be served as a side dish, but is also delicious as a main course, stuffed with the filling of your choice.

Serves 5

* 1kg white or yellow sweet potatoes, unpeeled
* 40g salt
* 80g manteiga de garrafa, clarified butter or ghee (see tip)
* 4 tbsp chopped spring onions (optional)

1. Preheat the oven to 200°C (400°F), gas mark 6. Scrub the potatoes under cold running water and pat dry. Rub their skins with the salt.

2. Wrap each potato in a piece of aluminium foil. Place the potatoes on a baking sheet and bake for 40 minutes until tender.

3. Remove from the oven and unwrap the potatoes, leaving the skin intact. Being careful not to get burned, squeeze the potatoes gently to force them open along the top, forming a slit lengthways.

4. Put a spoonful of manteiga de garrafa in each slit and sprinkle with the chopped spring onions, if using. Serve at once.

Tips from Thiago:
Manteiga de garrafa is sold in bottles from Brazilian stores, but you can make your own clarified butter substitute. Melt butter in a pan over a low heat, then skim off the froth from the surface. The butter will separate into two layers – carefully pour off and reserve the top clear yellow liquid and discard the milky bottom layer left behind.

Vegetais assados
Roasted vegetables

Roots, tubers and bulbs play an important role in Brazilian cuisine. Chayote (cho cho) is a fruit-vegetable that is part of the curcubitacea *family, along with melons, cucumbers, pumpkins and courgettes. According to historians, it was cultivated by the Aztecs and Mayans. Like the chayote, root vegetables and tubers were long considered poor food in Brazil, perhaps because of their abundance and easy cultivation. Nowadays, however, they are found in sophisticated and creative haute cuisine dishes such as Tuna Cannelloni with Chayote Tartare (see page 128).*

Serves 4

* salt
* 150g cassava root
* 200g starchy potatoes
* 100g chayote (cho cho)
* 2 tomatoes
* 200g winter squash
* 2 red onions
* 20ml extra virgin olive oil
* 2 thyme sprigs
* 1 rosemary sprig

1. Bring 1 litre of water to the boil in a saucepan with ½ tablespoon of salt. Peel the cassava, cut in half lengthways and then into 8cm logs. Add them to the boiling water and cook until tender. Drain and set aside.

2. Bring another 1 litre of water to the boil in a saucepan with ½ tablespoon of salt. Cut the potatoes into wedges and simmer for 20 minutes. Drain and set aside.

3. Cut the winter squash into 2cm-thick wedges. In another saucepan with 1 litre of water and ½ tablespoon of salt, cook the squash for 7 minutes. Drain and set aside.

4. Peel the chayote under cold running water, remove the seed and cut the flesh into 8 wedges. Bring 1 litre of water to the boil in a saucepan with ½ tablespoon of salt. Add the chayote and simmer for 5 minutes. Drain and set aside.

5. Cut each tomato into 4 wedges and season the lot with ½ teaspoon of salt. Cut each onion into 4 wedges.

6. Preheat the oven to 200°C (400°F), gas mark 6. Combine all the vegetables in a roasting tray. Drizzle with the olive oil, add the fresh herbs and bake for 12–15 minutes or until all the vegetables are light golden brown.

Tips from Thiago:
Use a brick oven if you have one, to give this recipe the most authentic flavour, and reduce the final cooking time to 5 minutes.

CASSAVA

Cassava (or manioc) is a native root that is the foundation of Brazilian culinary culture. There are more than 4,300 varieties catalogued in the country. Nowhere else in the world has a greater variety of flours and by-products made from one unique ingredient.

Farinha de tapioca 'bijuzada'
Farinha de tapioca substitute

Since farinha de tapioca is an ingredient not easily available outside Brazil and is yet integral to our cuisine, I have created this substitute. It uses polvilho doce (sweet cassava starch), which can be found in any Brazilian grocery store, as well as in some supermarkets and online.
Makes 500g

* 500g polvilho doce (sweet cassava starch)
* 3 litres filtered water

1. Put the starch in a large bowl and cover with the water. Leave to stand for 3 hours.

2. Carefully drain all the water from the bowl – the starch will remain at the bottom. Put the wet starch in the centre of a clean tea towel. Twist and squeeze the cloth to extract the excess water.

3. Pass the resulting dry mixture through a fine sieve, pressing down with the back of a spoon to create a powdery flour.

4. Preheat the oven to 150°C (300°F), gas mark 2. Meanwhile heat a wide, heavy-based frying pan over medium heat and sprinkle the starch over the base in a uniform layer. Cook until the granules start to stick together, forming a crepe-like disc. Flip it over and cook for 1 minute on the other side.

5. Remove from the pan and repeat with the remaining starch until it is all used up.

6. Use your hands to crush the starch discs to fine crumbs. Transfer to a baking tray and bake for 10 minutes or until crunchy. Cool, then store in an airtight container.

Farofa de castanha-do-pará
Savoury cassava flour crumble with Brazil nuts

Brazil nuts are known in Brazil as castanha-do-pará (literally, nuts from Pará). The tree is among the tallest in the Amazon rainforest, reaching heights of over 45 metres. The nuts are protected by a hard shell and further enclosed in a round, woody casing similar to a dried coconut. Each fruit contains 8–24 brazil nuts.

Serves 2

* 40g butter
* 70g Brazil nuts, coarsely chopped
* 200g Savoury Cassava Flour Crumble (see page 86)

1. Melt the butter in a large, heavy-based frying pan. Add the chopped nuts and cook for a few seconds, stirring.

2. Add the savoury cassava flour crumble and reduce the heat. Cook, stirring constantly, for a further 2 minutes. Remove from the heat and serve.

Tips from Thiago:
This farofa (pictured on page 85) is an excellent accompaniment to Smoked Arapaima in Coconut Milk (see page 122).

Savoury cassava flour crumble with banana

Savoury cassava flour crumble with eggs

Savoury cassava flour crumble with Brazil nuts

Savoury cassava flour crumble

FAROFA

One of the features of Brazilian cuisine is the love of having many different textures on one plate. Farofa is a favourite accompaniment for Brazilian dishes, adding crunchiness and comfort to dishes with rice, beans, fish and meat. Farofa is also used as a stuffing for roast chicken and turkey.

Farofa simples

Savoury cassava flour crumble

This is the classic, plain farofa – the most popular version throughout Brazil, from north to south.

Serves 2 (Makes about 300g)

* 100g butter
* 30g onion, chopped
* 200g extra fine, untoasted cassava flour
* ½ tsp salt

1. Melt the butter in a large, heavy-based frying pan and sauté the onion until translucent.

2. Stir in the cassava flour and salt. Reduce the heat and toast the mixture, stirring constantly, until it is light golden brown and crunchy.

Tips from Thiago:
If you use garlic instead of onion you will have a garlic farofa. Be careful not to burn the mixture – the trick is to toast it slowly over a very low heat.

Farofa de banana

Savoury cassava flour crumble with banana

The use of bananas in savoury dishes is a distinctive feature of Brazilian cookery – so too is farofa, a traditional side dish similar to a savoury crumble and made with toasted cassava flour. What we have here is a classic recipe combining both of them.

Serves 2

* 20g butter
* 10g onion, chopped
* 170g ripe banana, peeled and roughly chopped into large pieces
* 180g Savoury Cassava Flour Crumble (see left)
* 5g flat-leaf parsley, chopped
* 5g coriander leaves, chopped
* salt and black pepper

1. Melt the butter in a large frying pan and sauté the onion until tender and translucent. Add the banana and cook, stirring constantly, until it is slightly softened.

2. Add the savoury cassava flour crumble, parsley and coriander. Cook until everything has heated through.

3. Season to taste with salt and black pepper, then remove from the heat and serve.

Tips from Thiago:
This is the perfect accompaniment to fish grilled over hot coals.

Farofa
de ovo caipira
Savoury cassava flour crumble with eggs

In my home and the homes of many people from Pará, especially those living in the countryside, this easy egg farofa is a must at breakfast. It is also one of the most popular side dishes in our restaurant, to accompany both fish and meat dishes.

Serves 2

* 30g butter
* 20g onion, chopped
* 3 large free-range eggs
* salt and black pepper
* 180g farinha-d'água or toasted cassava flour
* 5g coriander leaves, chopped

1. Melt the butter in a frying pan and sauté the onion for 2 minutes or until translucent.

2. Break in the eggs, season with salt and pepper, stir, and cook for a further 2 minutes until the yolks start to set slightly.

3. Stir in the farinha-d'água and coriander. Remove from the heat and serve immediately.

Tips from Thiago:
You can also use Savoury Cassava Flour Crumble (see opposite) instead of farinha d' água.

Farofa de açaí
Savoury cassava flour crumble with açai

Serves 8

* 1kg raw cassava, peeled and cut into large pieces
* 500g açai pulp
* 100g unsalted butter
* ½ tsp salt

1. Put the cassava and açai together in a food processor and process for 5 minutes or until a paste is formed.

2. Pour the paste into a colander lined with a clean tea towel. Twist and squeeze the cloth to extract the juice, then discard the juice.

3. Pass the resulting dry mixture through a fine sieve, pressing down with the back of a spoon to create a flour.

4. Put the cassava and açai flour in a large, heavy-based frying pan and stir over a low heat for 20 minutes or until the mixture resembles dry breadcrumbs.

5. In a separate frying pan, melt the butter. Add the toasted cassava and açai flour, season with the salt and cook over a low heat for about 30 minutes, stirring constantly. Serve hot or cold.

Dried fish crumble

PAÇOCAS

Paçoca – in native Brazilian tupi dialect – means 'to crumble'. It is a dry preparation made of cassava flour and other ingredients such as dried meat, fish and nuts, all pounded together in a mortar. It is an accompaniment similar to farofa (see pages 86–7).

Brazilian jerk beef crumble

Cashew nut crumble

Paçoca de pirarucu seco
Dried fish crumble

In Brazil, the word paçoca refers to two distinct specialities. One of them is a traditional sweet peanut bar. The following recipes though are the savoury specialities of native Indians, served as side dishes.

Serves 5

* 200g salted pirarucu (arapaima) or salt cod fillets
* 500g fine, untoasted cassava flour
* 60g culantro (Mexican/long coriander)
* 40g red onion, roughly chopped
* salt

1. Cut the fish fillets into 1cm-wide strips, then soak in plenty of cold water for 24 hours, changing the water every 4 hours. (If using salt cod, soak for 24 hours before cutting into strips.)

2. Put the fish in a dehydrator at 68°C, or place on a baking tray and bake in the oven at 50°C (100°F), gas mark ⅛, for about 6 hours or until completely dry.

3. Using a large mortar and pestle, pound the fish, cassava flour, culantro and red onion until a coarse mealy mixture is obtained. Add salt, if needed. This is especially good served with Mullet Wrapped in Banana Leaf (see page 124).

Paçoca de carne-seca
Brazilian jerk beef crumble

Also known as paçoca de pilão, this paçoca is made of cassava flour and carne-seca – Brazil's version of jerk beef (see page 246). It can be used to accompany any hearty dish, such as the Bean Stew on page 193.

Serves 8

* 1kg carne-seca, cut into large cubes
* 300g red onion, finely sliced
* 200g manteiga de garrafa or clarified butter or ghee (see tip on page 76)
* 500g coarse farinha-d'água or toasted cassava flour
* 15g coriander leaves, chopped
* 20g spring onions, chopped
* salt

1. Put the carne-seca in a bowl, cover with cold water. Soak for 4 hours, changing the water every hour to remove the excess salt from the meat.

2. Preheat a charcoal barbecue. Meanwhile, drain the meat, and cook in a pressure cooker for 40 minutes or until it is fork tender (see tip, opposite). Transfer the beef to the barbecue and cook for about 20 minutes or until it has slightly dried out. Alternatively, place in a preheated oven at 130°C (275°F), gas mark 1, for 30 minutes. Set aside.

3. Heat 50g of the manteiga de garrafa in a frying pan and sauté the onion until softened. Set aside.

4. Using a large mortar and pestle, pound the dried meat with the farinha-d'água until the mixture resembles fresh breadcrumbs. Stir in the sautéed onion, the remaining manteiga de garrafa, the coriander and spring onions. Season to taste with salt, though you may find you don't need it.

Paçoca de castanha-de-caju
Cashew nut crumble

My grandparents used to live in Bragança, in the Pará countryside. Their house had a large back garden with several cashew trees. When the fruit was in season (December to January), my grandfather used to prepare this paçoca using the cashew nuts from his own trees. I can still remember the aroma of the nuts being roasted. The fresh cashew nuts were spread on an improvised baking sheet, pierced all over using a hammer and nail. This was then placed directly over a campfire. The nuts were roasted until their skins turned completely black. At this point, the skin was removed so we could eat the nuts – what a treat!

Serves 4

* 250g unsalted cashew nuts
* 250g farinha-d'água or toasted cassava flour
* 100g caster sugar
* 1 tsp salt

1. Using a large wooden mortar and pestle, pound the cashew nuts together with the farinha-d'água, sugar and salt until the mixture resembles fine, dry sand.

Tips from Thiago:
If you don't have a pressure cooker, cook the meat in the oven over a low heat for 1½ hours or until fork tender.

If you don't have a large enough mortar and pestle at home, you can make the paçoca in a blender or food processor. Follow the same procedure, pulsing the mixture until it resembles fine sand. You can also use salted cashews for this recipe, in which case omit the teaspoon of salt.

ARROZ

Maniçoba rice

Pará cress rice

Coconut rice

Rice with egg

Rice with dried salt shrimps

Arroz branco

Brazilian-style white rice

Rice is integral to Brazilian cuisine, serving as an accompaniment for countless dishes. Here is a recipe for basic, everyday rice.

Serves 2

* 100g long-grain white rice
* 1 tbsp vegetable oil
* 1 tbsp chopped onion
* ½ tsp chopped garlic
* salt

1. Rinse the rice several times in cold water, rubbing the grains against the palms of your hands inside a bowl, until the water turns clear. Drain thoroughly and let the rice dry before using.

2. Bring 200ml of water to the boil.

3. Heat the oil in a medium saucepan. Sauté the onion and the garlic until the onion is softened and the garlic light golden brown. Add the rice and cook, stirring constantly, until it becomes chalky.

4. Pour the boiling water onto the rice and bring to the boil again. Add a little salt and stir well. Half-cover the pan and cook over a medium-low heat until all the water has evaporated.

5. Turn off the heat and let the rice stand, covered, for about 10 minutes before serving.

Arroz com ovo

Rice with egg

Serves 4

* 25g butter
* 3 eggs
* salt and black pepper
* 200g hot Brazilian-style White Rice (see page 94)
* 1 tbsp finely chopped spring onions

1. Heat the butter in a large frying pan, break in the eggs and season to taste with salt and a pinch of pepper. Cook until the eggs start to set, then stir well and keep stirring as you let them finish cooking.

2. Add the prepared rice and spring onions. Stir well to combine and serve immediately.

Arroz de aviú

Rice with dried salt shrimps

Serves 4

* 40g unsalted butter
* 150g dried aviú (tiny dried, salty shrimps) or regular dried salt shrimps
* 200g hot Brazilian-style White Rice (see page 94)
* 30g culantro (Mexican/long coriander), or coriander leaves, coarsely chopped

1. Heat the butter in a large frying pan and sauté the aviú for 2 minutes.

2. Add the prepared rice and culantro and stir well to combine.

Arroz de coco

Coconut rice

The food historian and anthropologist, Câmara Cascudo, responsible for invaluable studies on Brazilian culture, once said that 'with coconut milk on it, one can eat sand' thus recognizing that this product is one of the most popular in our country. Coconut rice is much appreciated as an accompaniment in the northeast region, but mainly in Bahia. Most recipes use coconut milk. My version, however, is made with coconut water, coconut oil and shredded coconut.

Serves 4

* 400g long-grain white rice
* 40ml coconut oil
* 2 tbsp chopped onion
* 800ml coconut water
* 1 tbsp salt
* 70g unsweetened, finely shredded desiccated coconut

1. Put the rice in a sieve and rinse under cold running water.

2. Heat the coconut oil in a frying pan and sauté the onion until softened. Add the rice to the pan and cook, stirring, for 1 minute. Add the coconut water, salt and desiccated coconut.

3. Bring the mixture to the boil, then half-cover the pan, lower the heat and cook for 15 minutes or until the liquid has almost completely evaporated.

4. Turn off the heat and let the rice stand, covered, for 5 minutes. Serve hot.

Tips from Thiago:
Serve this as an accompaniment to Bahia-style Fish Stew (see page 134).

Arroz de jambu

Pará cress rice

Serves 4

* 200g jambu (Pará cress/toothache plant) or watercress
* 200g long-grain white rice
* 2 tbsp Brazil nut oil
* 30g onion, finely diced
* 1 tsp finely chopped garlic
* 400ml Tucupi substitute (see page 104)
* ½ tsp salt

1. Discard the tough parts of the jambu and set aside the tender leaves and stems.

2. Bring 1.5 litres of water to the boil in a saucepan. Add the jambu and cook until wilted. Using a slotted spoon, transfer the leaves immediately to a bowl of iced water to stop the cooking. Drain and set aside.

3. Rinse the rice, then drain it well and leave to dry. Heat 1 tablespoon of the Brazil nut oil in a saucepan. Add the onion and garlic and sauté for 2 minutes. Add the rice and sauté for a further 1 minute.

4. Stir in the tucupi substitute and salt. Cover the pan and cook for 15 minutes or until the rice is fluffy and moist.

5. Heat the remaining tablespoon of Brazil nut oil in a frying pan and sauté the wilted jambu for 1 minute. Add this to the cooked rice and stir well to combine. Serve immediately.

Tips from Thiago:
Extra virgin olive oil can be used as a substitute for the Brazil nut oil if necessary.

Arroz de maniçoba

Maniçoba rice

Serves 2

* 2 tbsp vegetable oil
* 1 tbsp chopped onion
* 100g long-grain white rice
* salt
* 200g prepared maniçoba (see page 46)
* 1 tbsp chopped culantro (Mexican/long coriander)

1. Heat the oil in a saucepan and fry the onion until softened. Add the rice and sauté for 1 minute.

2. Pour in 100ml boiling water and add a little salt, then cook over a low heat for 6 minutes or until virtually all the water has evaporated. Add the prepared maniçoba and continue cooking for a further 6 minutes.

3. Fold the culantro into the rice, then remove the pan from the heat. Cover and leave the rice to stand for 10 minutes before serving.

Manteiga defumada com cacau
Smoked butter with cocoa nibs

Serves 4

* 1 piece charcoal
* 10g sawdust suitable for smoking
* 100g salted butter
* 1 tsp cocoa nibs, finely chopped

1. Choose a metal bowl that fits inside a heavy-based saucepan with a tight-fitting lid. Light the charcoal and put it in the pan. Sprinkle the sawdust over the charcoal.

2. Put the butter in the metal bowl and place it in the pan. Cover immediately and seal the lid with cling film, to prevent the smoke escaping. Leave to stand for 30 minutes.

3. Remove the bowl of butter from the pan and stir in the chopped cocoa nibs.

4. Put some ice cubes and cold water in a large bowl and sit the bowl of butter inside it. Stir constantly with a spatula until the butter reaches the desired consistency. Store in the refrigerator. Best served slightly soft.

Manteiga de aviú
Dried salt shrimp butter

Serves 4

* 100g unsalted butter, at room temperature
* 2 tbsp dried aviú (tiny dried, salty shrimps) or finely chopped regular dried salt shrimps
* 1 tbsp double cream

1. Melt 50g of the butter in a frying pan and sauté the aviú over a low heat until golden brown.

2. Remove from the heat and whisk in the remaining butter and cream until combined. Store in the refrigerator. Best served slightly soft.

Manteiga de cumaru
Tonka bean butter

Serves 4

* ½ tonka bean
* 100g unsalted butter

1. Finely grate the tonka bean – I prefer to use a Microplane zester to do this.

2. Melt 50g of the butter in a frying pan. Add the grated tonka bean and cook for 2 minutes over a low heat.

3. Remove from the heat and whisk in the remaining butter until combined. Store in the refrigerator. Best served slightly soft.

Manteiga de castanha-de-caju

Cashew nut butter

Serves 6

* 200g unsalted butter, at room temperature
* 100g unsalted cashew nuts or walnuts

1. Preheat the oven to 160°C (325°F), gas mark 3. Spread the cashew nuts on a baking sheet and bake for 10 minutes or until golden brown. Remove from the oven and allow to cool a little.

2. Place the cashew nuts and the butter in a blender. Process for 1 minute until a smooth paste forms. Store in an airtight jar and serve at room temperature. It will keep for up to 2 weeks in the refrigerator.

Manteiga de coco tostado

Toasted coconut butter

Serves 6

* 40g unsweetened, finely shredded desiccated coconut
* 200g unsalted butter, at room temperature
* 30ml extra virgin coconut oil

1. Tip the shredded coconut into a small nonstick frying pan over a low heat. Toast slowly, stirring constantly, until golden brown. Remove from the heat and allow to cool.

2. Beat the butter, toasted coconut and coconut oil in a bowl until well blended. Store in an airtight jar and serve at room temperature. It will keep for up to 2 weeks in the refrigerator.

Toasted coconut butter

Cashew nut butter

Smoked butter with cocoa nibs

Dried salt shrimp butter

Tonka bean butter

Pepper jelly

Hot chillies
with tucupi

Coconut milk and
chilli sance

Pickled
cumari-do-Pará
chillies

Pickled kiss peppers

Pickled
smoked chillies

Geleia de pimenta

Pepper jelly

Serves 6 (Makes 1 x 250ml jar)

* 4 pimentas dedo-de-moça
  or other hot red chillies,
  deseeded and chopped
* 1 apple, peeled and coarsely grated
* 200g caster sugar
* 200ml orange juice
* 2 garlic cloves, peeled
* pinch of salt

1. Combine all the ingredients in a saucepan and cook over a low heat for 20 minutes.

2. Leave the mixture to cool completely then discard the garlic cloves.

3. Pour the jelly mixture into a sterilized glass jar and close the lid tightly. Store in the refrigerator.

Pimenta-cumari-do-pará no vinagre

Pickled cumari-do-pará chillies

Serves 4 (Makes 1 x 250ml jar)

* 125g coarse rock salt
* 100g cumari-do-pará or other mild chillies
* 250ml white wine vinegar
* 1 rosemary sprig
* 10 black peppercorns
* 1 garlic clove
* 20g root ginger, unpeeled, rinsed and sliced
* 1 bay leaf

1. Prepare a brine solution by combining 250ml of water with the coarse salt.

2. Rinse the chillies, add to the brine solution and leave to soak for 10 minutes.

3. Rinse the chillies under cold running water to remove the excess salt. Pat them dry and transfer to a sterilized glass jar.

4. Combine the vinegar, rosemary, peppercorns, garlic, ginger and bay leaf in a saucepan. Heat until almost boiling, then pour over the chillies. Close the lid tightly and let cool. Store in the refrigerator.

Pimenta defumada conservada no vinagre

Pickled smoked chillies

Serves 6 (Makes 1 x 350ml jar)

* 150g coarse rock salt
* 250g pimenta dedo-de-moça
  or other hot red chillies
* 350ml white wine vinegar

1. Prepare a brine solution by combining 500ml of water with the coarse salt.

2. Rinse the chillies, add to the brine and leave to soak for 10 minutes.

3. Rinse the chillies under cold running water to remove the excess salt. Pat dry and place on a metal strainer. Leave the strainer over a brick oven for 8 hours and close to the door, or use a smoker.

4. Put the chillies in a sterilized glass jar. Heat the vinegar to just below boiling point, then pour over the chillies to cover. Close the lid tightly and store in the refrigerator.

Molho de leite de coco com pimenta
Coconut milk and chilli sauce

This recipe is inspired by a typical sauce of Maranhão state. The original is made with pimenta-malagueta and babaçu milk – extracted from a nut produced by a palm tree found in the states of Maranhão, Mato Grosso, Piauí, Tocantins and Pará.

Serves 4 (Makes 1 x 250ml jar)

* 200ml unsweetened coconut milk
* 50g cumari-do-Pará chillies or other mild chilli peppers, deseeded and thinly sliced
* 1 garlic clove, unpeeled, crushed
* 2 tbsp white cachaça
* salt to taste

1. Heat the coconut milk to scalding point, then add the chillies, garlic, cachaça and salt to taste.

2. Remove from the heat and allow to cool completely. Discard the garlic clove and transfer to a sterilized glass jar with a tight fitting lid. Store in a refrigerator for up to 3 days.

Molho de pimenta com tucupi

Hot chillies with tucupi

Serves 8 (Makes 2 x 400ml jars)

* 250g cumari-do-Pará or other mild yellow chillies
* 25ml extra virgin olive oil
* 500ml Tucupi substitute (see page 104)
* 1 tsp chopped garlic
* 1 tbsp salt
* 25ml white cachaça

Conserva de pimenta-biquinho
Pickled kiss peppers

Although these peppers belong to the habanero family (Capsicum chinense) they have little heat and can even be eaten by themselves as a cocktail snack.

Serves 8 (Makes 2 x 400ml jars)

* 500ml white wine vinegar
* 40g sugar
* 1 clove garlic
* 2 bay leaves
* 300g kiss peppers or other small mild sweet peppers
* 70g salt

1. Place the vinegar, sugar, garlic and bay leaves in a saucepan and bring to the boil. Turn off the heat and let the mixture cool.

2. Rinse the peppers and put them in a bowl. Add the salt, stir and let stand for 2 hours.

3. Drain the peppers and rinse them to remove excess salt. Dry thoroughly. Divide them between sterilized glass jars, fill with the vinegar, leaving a 1cm gap below the lid. Seal and store in a refrigerator.

1. Rinse the chillies and discard the stems. Make small incisions in the skin of the chillies to allow the seasonings to penetrate.

2. Combine the oil, tucupi, garlic, salt and cachaça in a sterilized glass jar. Add the chillies and refrigerate. It will keep for up to 2 weeks.

Tucupi caseiro
Tucupi substitute

Tucupi is the most emblematic ingredient for cooking with in the state of Pará. This broth, originally yellow, is obtained by extracting the juice of an inedible raw cassava. Although poisonous when extracted, the liquid becomes a delicacy full of flavour after being cooked for many hours and then seasoned. Tucupi is a key ingredient in many dishes in this book, so I have created this alternative using regular, non-poisonous cassava, so that you can prepare it safely at home.

Makes 2 litres

* 4kg raw cassava, peeled and cubed
* 1 tbsp salt
* 2 garlic cloves, unpeeled
* 4 tbsp hand-torn coriander sprigs
* 2 tbsp chopped basil leaves

Tips from Thiago:
This broth can be refrigerated for up to 5 days, or frozen for up to 30 days. The goma de mandioca can be saved and put to use in other recipes.

1. Put the cubed cassava in a blender. Turn it on and gradually add 1.5 litres of water, processing until a paste is formed.

2. Pour the paste into a colander lined with a clean, thickly woven tea towel. Working over a bowl, twist the tea towel into a bundle, pressing the contents with your hands to extract the juices from the cassava paste. Leave the liquid to stand in the bowl for 3 hours.

3. Strain the liquid that has pooled on the top into a separate bowl, leaving behind the starch at the bottom of the bowl (this is the goma de mandioca).

4. Cover the bowl of liquid with a clean tea towel and leave to ferment at room temperature for 24 hours. The liquid will start to froth and release a sour smell.

5. Transfer the fermented juice to a saucepan and add the salt, garlic, coriander and basil. Bring to the boil and simmer for 40 minutes.

6. Pass the mixture through a sieve, then leave to cool before storing in the refrigerator in a covered bowl.

VER-O-PESO

This is the largest open food market in Latin America, surrounded by historic buildings, and covering an area of 35,000 square metres by Guajará Bay. In 1977 it was declared a part of Brazil's national heritage. The name means 'look at the weight', as there are large scales available for buyers and sellers to verify the weight of the produce. The market receives fresh native fish from the Amazon daily, as well as native vegetables, fruits and medicinal herbs from the rainforest.

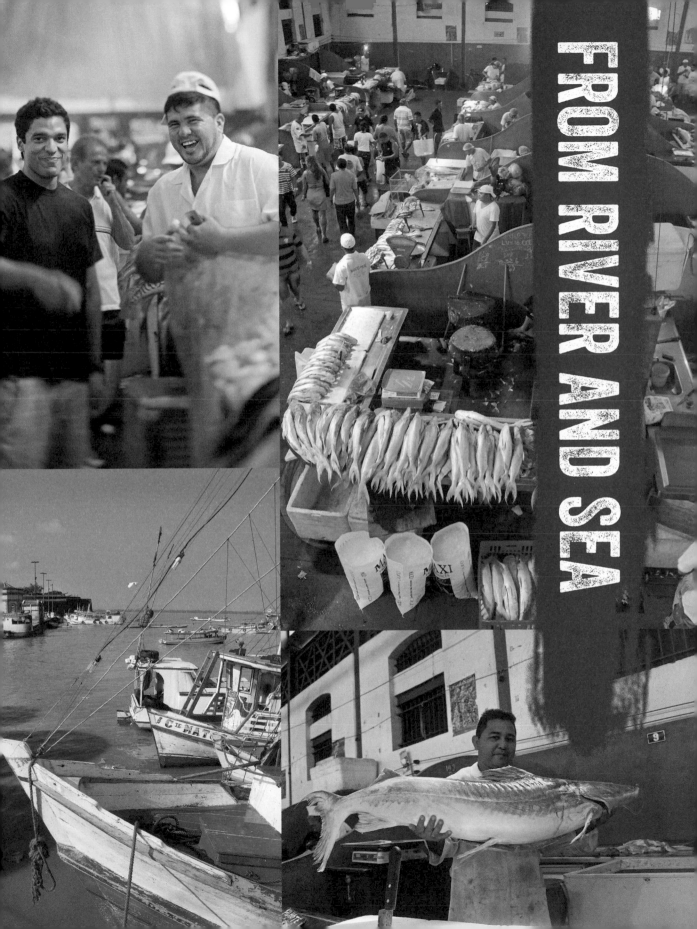

FROM RIVER AND SEA

Caldeirada de filhote
Pará-style fish stew

This is one of the most emblematic dishes of the Brazilian Amazon. Pará-style caldeirada has indigenous origins, but there are other versions in Galician and Portuguese cuisines that have their own distinctive recipes. In Brazil, there are regional variations, too, using different seasonings, fish and shellfish or even meat. This is how we prepare and serve it at our restaurant – with plenty of broth, and accompanied by pirão, a dish of fish stock thickened with cassava flour.

Serves 4

* 2.5 litres Fish Stock (see page 132)
* 2 free-range eggs
* 600g filhote or catfish steaks (loin), or hake or halibut fillets
* juice of 2 limes
* salt and freshly ground white pepper
* 5 tbsp olive oil
* 2 tbsp chopped onion, plus 100g whole, small cooking onions, peeled
* 2 tbsp chopped tomato, plus 80g whole, small ripe tomatoes
* 1 tbsp chopped pimenta-de-cheiro or other mild chilli
* 100g potatoes, peeled and cut into large cubes
* 50g yellow pepper, cut into large squares
* 50g green pepper, cut into large squares
* 50g red pepper, cut into large squares
* 2 tbsp hand-torn culantro (Mexican/ long coriander)
* 1 tbsp chopped coriander leaves
* 2 tbsp hand-torn basil

Fish pirão
* 30ml olive oil
* 20g onion, chopped
* 20g tomato, chopped
* 100g small, peeled shrimps
* juice of 1 lime
* 100g fine cassava flour
* 1 tbsp chopped coriander leaves

1. Prepare the fish stock (see the Fish and Prawn Soup recipe on page 132, steps 1–3), but do not use the prawn shells and heads, and add 3 litres of water instead of 2 litres. When the stock is ready, set aside 2 litres to use in the stew and 500ml to make the pirão.

2. Carefully lower the eggs into a pan of boiling water and cook for 7 minutes. Drain and cool under cold running water, then peel and set aside.

3. Put the fish steaks in a large bowl and season with the lime juice, salt and white pepper. Leave to marinate in the refrigerator for 20 minutes.

4. Meanwhile, start the pirão. Heat the olive oil in a medium saucepan and sauté the onion and tomato. Add the shrimps, the 500ml fish stock and the lime juice. Bring to the boil. Lower the heat and sprinkle in the cassava flour in a steady flow, constantly stirring with a whisk to prevent lumps forming, and cook until the mixture is the consistency of hot polenta.

5. To cook the caldeirada, heat 1 tablespoon of the olive oil in a large pot (preferably made of clay) and sauté the chopped onion, chopped tomato and chilli until wilted.

6. Add the fish, potatoes, whole onions, whole tomatoes, yellow, green and red peppers, culantro, coriander leaves, basil and the 2 litres of fish stock. Boil for 8 minutes or until the fish flakes and is cooked through.

7. Add the boiled eggs to the pan and drizzle with the remaining olive oil. Sprinkle the pirão with the cilantro leaves and serve with Brazilian-style White Rice (see page 94).

Filhote assado na brasa

Chargrilled filhote

This recipe is a memory of my childhood. My father often prepared it at home, and it became one of the most popular dishes in our first restaurant, Remanso do Peixe.

Serves 2

* 50ml dry white wine
* juice of 2 limes
* 20g salt
* ½ tsp ground black pepper
* 500g filhote tranche or sea bass fillets
* 1 tbsp melted butter

1. Combine the white wine, lime juice, salt and black pepper in a bowl with 1 litre of water. Add the fish, cover and leave to marinate in the refrigerator for 2 hours.

2. Preheat a charcoal barbecue and fish grill basket. Discard the marinade and put the fish in the grill basket. Sit it 40cm above the hot coals and chargrill for 7 minutes on each side (less for the sea bass fillets) or until the surface is golden brown and the flesh tender.

3. Finish by brushing the fish with the melted butter.

Tips from Thiago:
Serve with Roasted Vegetables (see page 78).

Camurim marinado no tucupi
White snook ceviche with tucupi dressing

In Peru I learned how to make the famous tiger milk, used to marinate ceviches. But don't worry – to prepare this recipe, you will not need to go in search of this exotic feline! This delicious, classic Andean sauce of milky appearance is made with fish scraps, lemon and aji pepper. In my recipe, I have adopted the same principles of the original recipe, but added an ingredient from my region: tucupi.

Serves 2

* 200ml tucupi or Tucupi substitute (see page 104)
* 160g white snook or cod fillets, plus 40g fish scraps (bones, head, tail)
* 100ml lime juice
* 10g garlic, crushed
* 50g root ginger, chopped
* 50g onion, chopped
* 5g salt
* 6 ice cubes
* 10g coriander stems
* 1 yellow pimenta-de-cheiro or other mild yellow chilli

To serve

* 5g buzz buttons (Pará cress flower buds), stems removed
* 5g coriander leaves
* 1 cumari-do-Pará or other mild yellow chilli, finely sliced
* sea salt flakes

1. Combine the tucupi, fish scraps, lime juice, garlic, ginger, onion, salt and the ice cubes in a blender. Process until smooth.

2. Add the coriander stems and pimenta-de-cheiro and pulse briefly to combine but prevent the chilli and coriander from releasing their colour into the mixture. Keep refrigerated.

3. Cut the fish fillets against the grain into fine slices and keep refrigerated.

4. Spoon the tucupi dressing onto a serving plate. Arrange some slices of fish on top and sprinkle with the flowers and coriander leaves. Finish by putting a slice of chilli on each slice of fish. Sprinkle with some sea salt flakes and serve.

Tips from Thiago:
Keep all the components of this dish well chilled until ready to serve.

Costela de tambaqui na brasa
Chargrilled fish ribs

Tambaqui is the second largest fish with scales in Brazil. This Amazon giant can reach 2 metres in length and weigh more than 30 kilos. When fatty, its meat resembles pork. For this recipe we are using tambaqui ribs, one of the cuts that I like the most.

Serves 3

* 15g salt
* 4 black peppercorns
* 3 garlic cloves, crushed
* 30ml olive oil
* 3 racks of tambaqui ribs, about 250g each, or other fatty fish such as salmon
* 100g melted butter, for brushing

1. Using a mortar and pestle, pound together the salt, peppercorns, garlic and the olive oil to form a paste.

2. Spread the mixture all over the fish racks, cover and leave to marinate in the refrigerator for 40 minutes. Meanwhile, preheat a charcoal barbecue.

3. Sit the fish racks about 30cm above the hot coals. Brush the fish with melted butter and chargrill for 6 minutes on each side or until the fish is golden brown and cooked through.

Tips from Thiago:
To enjoy a tambaqui you will have to pay us a visit in Brazil – it is a unique experience! But you can also make this recipe using the ribs of salmon or catfish, or use the recipe to prepare pork ribs. A delicious and healthy side dish to serve with this recipe is the Bean and Okra Salad (see page 70).

Pirarucu no leite de castanha-do-pará

Arapaima with Brazil nut milk

Brazil nuts are a high protein food and can be consumed in various ways. The milk made from them can be used as a substitute for coconut milk or cows' milk, and gives a delicious flavour to recipes. It is a great alternative for lactose-intolerant people.

Serves 2

* 300g raw Brazil nuts
* 2 fresh pirarucu (arapaima) or cod fillets, about 200g each, skin on
* salt and black pepper
* 2 tbsp coarsely chopped culantro (Mexican/long coriander)
* 60g winter squash, cut into 5mm slices
* 1 red onion, quartered
* 60g okra, halved lengthways
* 60g West Indian gherkin or small cucumber, cut in half lengthways
* 60g mandioquinha (arracacha/Peruvian parsnip) or parsnip, cut into 1cm rounds
* 60g sweet potato, unpeeled, cut into 1cm rounds
* 60g tomato, quartered
* 3–4 sprigs of thyme, to serve

1. Put the Brazil nuts in a blender with 400ml of water and process for 5 minutes. Refrigerate for 30 minutes, then strain through a fine sieve and set aside (see tip, below).

2. Season the fish with salt and pepper and leave to stand for 30 minutes.

3. In a large saucepan, combine 1 litre of water and 1 tablespoon of salt and bring to the boil. Cook, separately, the sweet potato (for 5 minutes) and the mandioquinha (for 3 minutes) until al dente. Drain and set aside.

4. Preheat the oven to 220°C (425°F), gas mark 7. Put the fish fillets in a baking dish. Add the Brazil nut milk, culantro, squash, red onion, okra, West Indian gherkin, mandioquinha, sweet potato and tomato. Sprinkle the vegetables with ½ teaspoon of salt.

5. Bake for 10 minutes until the fish and the vegetables are cooked through and tender, then remove from the oven, scatter over the thyme and serve.

Tips from Thiago:
The ground Brazil nuts left after straining the milk can be used to make cakes, pies and biscuits.

Patas de caranguejo no vapor com vinagrete de abacate

Steamed crab claws with avocado salsa

During my childhood, we often used to visit Bragança, a city in the state of Pará. On the road to the beach were signs alerting us to crabs crossing the road. We had to stop the car many times to let them get to the other side and into the mangrove swamp. Several species of crab are at risk of extinction, so make sure you are buying from trusted suppliers. In that way you can keep having the pleasure of consuming this ever-so special crustacean and, at the same time, help with its preservation.

Serves 2

* 200g diced avocado flesh
* ½ cumari-do-Pará or other fresh chilli, deseeded and finely chopped
* 20g red onion, finely chopped
* 15g red pepper, diced
* 5g coriander leaves, coarsely chopped
* 10ml lime juice
* 20ml avocado oil
* salt and black pepper
* 150g peeled crab claws

Tips from Thiago:
When substituting the cumari-do-Pará chilli, be careful not to choose one that is too fierce. If using a hotter chilli, such as a bird's-eye chilli, reduce the amount accordingly.

1. Combine the avocado, chilli, onion, red pepper, coriander, lime juice and avocado oil in a bowl with 1 teaspoon of salt and some pepper. Mix gently and refrigerate until needed.

2. Season the crab claws with salt and black pepper and leave to stand for 10 minutes. Cook the claws in a steamer for 1 minute, then remove from the heat and set aside.

3. Drain the liquid from the avocado salsa. Pile 1 teaspoon of salsa on one side of a long, rectangular dish and lean a crab claw against it. Repeat the procedure with the remaining salsa and crab, forming a line along the centre of the plate.

Arroz de 'frutos do rio' com feijão-caupi e leite de coco

'Riverfood' risotto with black-eyed beans and coconut milk

This is a home-style recipe and every family has its own version. Coconut milk is a typical ingredient of the north and northeast regions of Brazil and is used to cook rice, fish and seafood dishes.

Serves 6

* 100g dried black-eyed beans, rinsed and sorted
* 200g sarnabi or other clams
* 200g shelled charru mussels or other mussels
* 200g whole freshwater prawns
* 200g squid rings
* 200g crab meat, shredded
* 100g peeled crab claws
* salt and pepper
* 5 tbsp coconut oil
* 4 tbsp chopped onion
* 2 tbsp chopped red pepper
* 2 tbsp chopped yellow pepper
* 2 tbsp chopped green pepper
* 2 tbsp chopped tomato
* 1 tbsp chopped garlic
* 2 tbsp chopped pimenta-de-cheiro or other mild chilli
* 100g bacon lardons (optional)
* 230g long-grain white rice
* 200ml unsweetened coconut milk
* 100g dried salt shrimps
* 300ml Fish Stock (see page 133)
* 1 tbsp chopped flat-leaf parsley
* 2 tbsp coriander leaves

Tips from Thiago:
This recipe can be adapted to any type of shellfish. Use the seafood that you like the most.

1. Soak the beans in plenty of cold water to cover for at least 6 hours or overnight. Drain the beans, put them in a pot and add fresh water to cover by 5cm. Cook over a low heat for 1 hour or until tender, but still firm to the bite. Drain and set aside.

2. Season all the fresh shellfish with salt and pepper, keeping them separate. Leave to stand for 8 minutes.

3. Heat the coconut oil in a large frying pan. Add the onion, the red, yellow and green peppers, tomato, garlic, chilli and bacon (if using) and sauté until golden brown.

4. Add the rice to the pan and sauté, stirring, for 1 minute. Stir in the cooked beans. Add the squid to the pan, sauté briefly, then add the coconut milk. Cook, stirring often, for 10 minutes.

5. Add the dried shrimps and fresh prawns, then the shredded crab meat, sarnabi, charru mussels and crab claws. Add the fish stock little by little, as needed. Adjust the salt while there is still liquid in the pan and add more if necessary.

6. Cover and cook over a low heat until the rice and seafood are cooked through, but still firm to the bite. Discard any mussels and clams that have not opened. Sprinkle with the coriander and parsley. Remove from the heat, cover and let sit for 3 minutes before serving.

Pirarucu defumado com leite de coco

Smoked arapaima in coconut milk

Records of the Pará-born historian, José Veríssimo, dating from 1895 claim that the pirarucu (arapaima) was the base of Amazonian food. That has not changed to the present day, as this fish is still characteristic of the region. Indigenous communities and Europeans both used salt-curing techniques to preserve it. In Pará, the pirarucu is usually salt-cured, but for this dish we are using the smoked version.

Serves 4

* 800g smoked pirarucu (arapaima) or smoked haddock fillets
* 20ml extra virgin olive oil
* 3 plantains, peeled and halved lengthways
* 3 tbsp chopped onion
* 2 tbsp finely diced red peppers, plus a few finely sliced rings
* 2 tbsp finely diced yellow peppers
* 1 tbsp finely diced green peppers, plus a few finely sliced rings
* 1 tbsp coriander leaves
* 1 tbsp chopped culantro (Mexican/long coriander)
* 1 tsp finely chopped garlic
* 600ml unsweetened coconut milk
* 5 prunes, pitted

1. Cut the fish into 1cm-wide strips. Heat 10ml of the olive oil in a nonstick frying pan and sear the fish strips on all sides until golden brown. Remove to a plate and set aside.

2. In the same pan, sear the halved plantains until golden brown. Set aside.

3. Heat the remaining olive oil in a large pot, preferably made of clay, and sauté the onion, the diced and sliced red, yellow and green peppers, coriander leaves, culantro and garlic for 2 minutes.

4. Stir in the coconut milk, prunes and smoked fish. Cook for 15 minutes over a low heat. Add the plantain and cook for a further 5 minutes. Remove from the heat and serve.

Tips from Thiago:
Serve with Brazilian-style White Rice (see page 94) or Pará Cress Rice (see page 96) and Savoury Cassava Flour Crumble with Brazil Nuts (see page 82).

Tainha assada na folha de bananeira
Mullet wrapped in banana leaf

The flavour and aroma of toasted banana leaves is an important culinary characteristic of Pará and the Amazon region. We like to wrap roasts in banana leaves, especially fish, to protect them from excessive heat during baking and, at the same time, infuse the food with their aroma.

Serves 2

* 15g salt
* 6 black peppercorns
* 2 garlic cloves, lightly crushed
* 30ml olive oil
* 2 whole mullet (or trout), about 800g each, cleaned and gutted
* 1 large banana leaf

1. Using a mortar and pestle, pound together the salt, peppercorns, garlic and olive oil to form a paste.

2. Remove the viscera and gills from the fish. Spread the garlic paste over the entire surface of the fish, inside and out. Place in a baking dish, cover and leave to marinate in the refrigerator for 40 minutes.

3. Preheat a charcoal barbecue. To prevent the banana leaf from tearing when wrapping the fish, wave it quickly over an open flame, just until it wilts slightly – you'll immediately see it changing colour and becoming more flexible.

4. Remove the fish from the refrigerator. Wrap it in the banana leaf so that the flesh is completely enclosed.

5. Place the parcel in a fish grill basket and sit it 30cm above the hot coals of the barbecue. Chargrill for 15 minutes on each side or until the fish is cooked through. Don't worry if the outer layer gets a little charred – the fish won't get burned, and the scorched leaf will lend a delicate bouquet to its flesh.

Tips from Thiago:
If you don't have a barbecue, you can cook the fish in the oven. Place the parcel on a grill rack in a roasting tray to prevent it touching the surface of the dish and bake at 200°C (400°F), gas mark 6 for 30 minutes.

Casquinha de caranguejo
Brazilian-style dressed crab

In Portuguese, there are two words for crab – siri and caranguejo. The difference is in the back legs, which look like fins or oars on the siri. This traditional Brazilian appetizer, served in tents on the beach and in the restaurants of large cities, is usually made with siri. However, this version uses caranguejo, which is much more common in the Bragança region, from where my mother comes.

Serves 4

* 100ml extra virgin olive oil
* 100g onion, finely chopped
* 30g garlic, finely chopped
* 800g crab meat, picked over
* 1 tsp salt
* pinch of black pepper
* 40g flat-leaf parsley, finely chopped
* 4–8 tbsp Savoury Cassava Flour Crumble (see page 86), hot or cold

1. Heat the olive oil in a saucepan. Add the onion and garlic and sauté for 1 minute.

2. Stir in the crab meat and sauté for 6 minutes over a low heat. Add the salt, pepper and parsley, then remove from the heat.

3. Stuff 4 clean crab shells with the crab mixture and cover with the cassava flour crumble – you can use as much as you want, but a tablespoon over each crab should be enough. Serve with lime wedges.

Tips from Thiago:
Substitute coriander for the parsley if you prefer.

Roberta Sudbrack

Canelone de atum e tartare de chuchu

Tuna cannelloni with chayote tartare

Serves 8

* 200g day-old bread, preferably sourdough
* filtered water
* 2 organic chayotes (cho cho), plus 4 extra to serve (optional)
* sea salt flakes
* caster sugar
* 3 tbsp extra virgin olive oil
* cayenne pepper
* 100g unsalted butter
* 30g flaked almonds
* 300g fresh tuna steak
* 1 tbsp dark treacle

1. The day before serving, cut the bread into cubes, sprinkle with filtered water, place in a sealed container and refrigerate overnight.

2. Next day, peel the 2 chayotes under cold running water, remove the pits and dice finely. Cook briefly in salted boiling water, then drain and plunge immediately into a bowl of iced water to stop the cooking and preserve the texture. Season to taste with sea salt flakes, sugar, olive oil and a little cayenne pepper. Refrigerate until well chilled.

3. Heat the butter in a wide pan and fry the cubed bread and almonds until golden brown. Season with a pinch of sugar. Drain in a sieve, then drain the bread and almonds on kitchen paper to absorb the excess fat.

4. Put the bread and almonds in a food processor and pulse until a mealy texture is obtained. Season with sea salt flakes and some extra sugar, if necessary – the flavour should be between sweet and savoury.

5. Finely slice the tuna steak. Place each slice between two sheets of clingfilm and bash until thin using the flat side of a meat mallet. Place a small quantity of the chayote tartare over each slice of tuna and carefully roll into a cannelloni-shaped log.

6. Whisk the treacle with some olive oil to obtain a vinaigrette-like mixture. Balance the sweetness by adding a pinch of sea salt.

7. If using chayotes to serve, chop the remaining 4 chayotes in half lengthways and remove the pits. Mound the bread and almond crumbs on each chayote half, place a cannelloni on top of each serving and finish with a drizzle of the treacle vinaigrette.

Bobó de camarão
Cassava and shrimp stew

This delicious, easy stew is one of the most famous dishes of Bahia and, like many other recipes of this state, has African origins. It is also prepared as an offering for religious ceremonies dedicated to the African deities, the Orixás. In African-Brazilian religions, each Orixá has its own preferred foods. In Candomblé, shrimp bobó is offered to the goddess Oxum, the queen of all rivers and waterfalls.

Serves 4

* 375ml coconut water
* 150g dried coconut meat
* 50g young (green) coconut meat
* 500g cassava root, peeled and cut into large pieces
* 30ml dendê (palm) oil
* 50g onion, finely chopped
* 1 tbsp chopped garlic
* 50g tomato, chopped
* 100g dried salt shrimps
* 20g pimenta-de-cheiro or other mild chilli, chopped
* 30g red pepper, cut into large squares
* 30g yellow pepper, cut into large squares
* 500g raw peeled prawns, with tails
* salt and black pepper
* juice of 1 lime
* 1 tbsp coarsely chopped coriander sprigs
* 1 tbsp coarsely chopped basil
* 1 tbsp coarsely chopped culantro (Mexican/long coriander)
* 1 tbsp chopped spring onion

Spice paste

* ½ tsp ground black pepper
* ½ tsp ground turmeric
* ½ tbsp finely chopped root ginger
* pinch of ground cumin
* 10ml annatto (achiote) oil
* ¼ hot red chilli, deseeded
* 2 tbsp peeled dried salt shrimps

1. Make the spice paste first. Combine all the ingredients in a blender or food processor and blend to a paste. Transfer to an airtight jar and store in the refrigerator.

2. Warm the coconut water in a saucepan. Put it in a blender with the dried coconut meat and process until the coconut pieces are very finely chopped. Strain through a fine sieve then return it to the blender. Add the young (green) coconut meat, blend until smooth and creamy and set aside.

3. Cook the cassava until tender in a large saucepan with enough water to cover. Drain and set aside.

4. Heat the dendê oil in a medium pot, preferably one made of clay, and sauté the onion, garlic, tomato, dried shrimps, pimenta-de-cheiro, red and yellow peppers and 1 tablespoon of the spice paste.

5. Stir in the coconut milk cream, bring to the boil and cook for 5 minutes. Remove from the heat and add the cooked cassava. Purée the contents of the pot with an immersion blender until smooth and creamy. Return to the heat.

6. Season the prawns with salt, pepper and lime juice and add them to the pot. Cook for 4 minutes until they turn pink and are cooked through. Add the fresh herbs and spring onion and serve hot with Coconut Rice (see page 95).

Tips from Thiago:
The spice paste can be made well in advance and keeps in the refrigerator for up to 2 weeks. If you cannot find the ingredients to make your own coconut milk cream, use ready-made unsweetened coconut milk instead.

Mojica de peixe
Fish and prawn soup

Traditionally from the Pantanal region, this dish is also of native Indian origin, and quite popular in Belém. It consists of a very flavourful and spicy broth thickened with cassava flour. You can use any kind of fish, as well as shrimps or aviú.

Serves 2

Fish stock
* 1kg heads of white fish
* 50ml lime juice
* salt
* 50ml extra virgin olive oil
* 60g onion, finely chopped
* 1 tbsp chopped pimenta-de-cheiro or other mild chilli
* 1 head garlic, about 20g, peeled and crushed
* 400g prawn heads and shells
* 2 tbsp chopped coriander stems
* 2 tbsp hand-torn culantro (Mexican/long coriander)
* 2 tbsp hand-torn basil

Mojica
* 40ml extra virgin olive oil
* 50g onion, chopped
* 50g tomato, chopped
* 1 tbsp chopped pimenta-de-cheiro or other mild chilli
* 1 tsp chopped garlic
* 1 cumari-do-Pará, or other mild yellow chilli, crushed
* 30g dried aviú (tiny dried, salty shrimps) or chopped regular dried salt shrimps
* 100g small freshwater prawns
* 100g fine cassava flour
* 1 tbsp chopped coriander leaves

1. To make the fish stock, put the fish heads in a bowl, drizzle with the lime juice and sprinkle with 60g of salt. Cover, and leave to marinate in the refrigerator for 30 minutes. Rinse the fish heads thoroughly under cold running water and set aside.

2. In a large pot, heat the olive oil and sauté the onion, chilli and garlic until softened. Add the fish heads and the prawn heads and shells, plus 2 litres of cold water. Stir in the fresh herbs and cook for 40 minutes.

3. Season the stock to taste with salt. Pass it through a sieve and keep warm. Remove the flesh attached to the fish heads and reserve it – you'll need about 100g.

4. To make the mojica, heat the olive oil in a large saucepan. Add the onion, tomato, pimenta-de-cheiro, garlic and cumari-do-Pará and cook until softened.

5. Stir in the aviú, prawns and reserved fish and sauté for 30 seconds. Pour in 1 litre of the hot fish stock, bring to the boil, and lower the heat to medium.

6. Add the cassava flour very slowly in a steady stream, stirring constantly with a whisk to prevent lumps forming. Cook for 5 minutes or until thickened.

7. Add the coriander and cook for a further 1 minute before removing the pan from the heat and serving, preferably in gourd bowls.

Tips from Thiago:
The consistency of mojica should be a thin, runny porridge-like texture.

Moqueca baiana
Bahia-style fish stew

De rio e mar } From river and sea

This stew is one of the most famous dishes of Brazil and, as its name implies, is traditional to Bahia state. It is prepared with coconut cream and dendê oil and served on a moquequeira (a clay dish made specially for serving moquecas). I usually make this with one of the most popular fish of our region, the filhote.

Serves 4

Spice paste
* 6 black peppercorns
* 1 tsp ground turmeric
* 10g root ginger
* 6 coriander seeds
* ½ pimenta malagueta or hot red chilli, deseeded
* 20g dried salt shrimps

Coconut cream
* 900ml coconut water
* 420g dried coconut meat
* 240g young (green) coconut meat

* 550g filhote or catfish steaks, or hake or halibut fillets
* juice of ½ lime
* salt
* 20ml dendê (palm) oil
* 30g onion, chopped, plus 30g onion, sliced
* 30g tomato, chopped, plus 30g tomato, sliced
* 5g garlic, crushed
* 3 pimentas-de-cheiro or other mild chillies
* 30g red pepper, sliced
* 20g green pepper, sliced
* 5g coriander leaves, roughly chopped
* 5g spring onions, finely chopped

1. First make the spice paste, process the black peppercorns, turmeric, ginger, coriander seeds, chilli and dried shrimp in a blender or food processor until a smooth paste forms. Transfer to an airtight container and store in the refrigerator for up to 10 days.

2. To make a coconut cream, warm the coconut water in a saucepan. Put it in a blender with the dried coconut meat and process until the coconut pieces are very finely chopped. Strain through a fine sieve, then return it to the blender. Add the young (green) coconut meat, blend until smooth and creamy and set aside.

3. Season the fish with the lime juice and a little salt and set aside.

4. In a large clay pot, heat the dendé oil over a medium heat and sauté the chopped onion, chopped tomato, garlic, pimentas-de-cheiro and 1 tablespoon of the spice paste until the vegetables are softened.

5. Stir in 1.1 litres of the coconut cream, bring to a simmer, then add the fish and cook for 5 minutes.

6. Add the red and green peppers and the tomato and onion slices and cook for a further 5 minutes. Sprinkle with the coriander and spring onions before serving.

Tips from Thiago:
Dendê oil and dried salt shrimps are sold in Brazilian and African stores. Substitute a good-quality shop-bought coconut milk for the coconut cream recipe if you can't find young (green) coconut meat to make it fresh.

My father learned how to cook as a child and this 'survival tool' came in very handy when he found himself without a job and had to find money to feed us. He first sold takeaway pizzas, but later his customers (mostly neighbours) asked him to cook classic dishes (see A Family Story on page 8).

Seu Chicão (his nickname) was raised in the countryside near Belém and learned most of his recipes from his parents. As he gained in experience, he started to improve the traditional dishes, adding his own touches, until eventually he began to create new and original dishes. Moqueca Paraense is one of his iconic specialities. He is not just my personal food hero, but also an important figure in the history of Brazilian cuisine.

Moqueca paraense
Pará-style moqueca

This dish was created and patented by my father, Seu Chicão, to become a classic of our region. It is the best-selling dish in our restaurant, Remanso do Peixe, and lots of people come from far away just to try it.

Serves 2

* 2 eggs
* 550g filhote or hake or halibut steaks
* salt and black pepper
* 1 tsp chopped garlic
* juice of ½ lime
* 50ml extra virgin olive oil, plus extra for drizzling
* 3 tbsp goma de mandioca (see tips, below)
* 1 litre tucupi or Tucupi substitute (see page 104)
* 30g onion, finely chopped, plus 30g onion, sliced
* 30g tomato, diced, plus 30g tomato, sliced
* 1 pimenta-de-cheiro or other mild chilli
* 30g red pepper, sliced
* 20g green pepper, sliced
* 2 tbsp coarsely chopped coriander leaves
* 2 tbsp chopped basil
* 2 tbsp chopped spring onions
* 100g cooked peeled prawns, with tails

1. Cook the eggs in a pan of simmering water for 8 minutes or until they are hard-boiled. Leave to cool, drain, then peel the eggs and cut in half. Set aside.

2. Season the fish with salt, black pepper, the garlic, lime juice and a drizzle of olive oil. Set aside.

3. Dissolve the goma de mandioca in 100ml of the tucupi and set aside.

4. Heat the 50ml of olive oil in a clay pot and sauté the finely chopped onion, diced tomato and pimenta-de-cheiro until softened.

5. Add the fish and remaining 900ml of tucupi to the pot. Cook for 5 minutes.

6. Add the mixture of goma de mandioca and tucupi to the pot, stirring well to combine. Cook until thickened.

7. Add the red and green peppers, sliced tomato, sliced onion and shrimps. Push the egg halves into the stew, sprinkle with the fresh herbs and spring onions and serve at once.

Tips from Seu Chicão
The goma de mandioca can be replaced by polvilho doce (sweet cassava starch) or cornflour. Serve this stew accompanied by Pará Cress Rice (see page 96) and fine, raw cassava flour.

Tucunaré com recheio de caranguejo e camarão

Peacock bass stuffed with crab and prawns

This dish was created by my father, inspired by a family recipe my grandfather used to make. The original recipe used a bone-in fish stuffed with banana farofa, but my father decided to de-bone the fish and fill it with crab meat and shrimps.

Serves 8

* 1 peacock bass or large sea bass, about 4.5kg, cleaned and gutted
* 200ml dry white wine vinegar
* juice of 3 limes
* 50ml extra virgin olive oil
* 1 tbsp finely chopped garlic
* 30g salt
* black pepper

Sauce

* 100g butter
* 60g onion, thinly sliced
* 60g red pepper, sliced
* 60g tomato, sliced
* 200ml Fish Stock (see page 133)
* 1 tbsp ground annatto (achiote)
* 1 tsp ground turmeric
* 2 tbsp flat-leaf parsley, finely chopped
* 1 tbsp chopped culantro (Mexican/long coriander)
* 100g raw peeled prawns, with tails

Filling

* 100ml extra virgin olive oil
* 30g onion, finely chopped
* 30g red pepper, chopped
* 30g tomato, diced
* 800g crab meat, picked over
* 800g raw peeled prawns, chopped
* 1 tbsp chopped flat-leaf parsley
* 2 tbsp chopped coriander leaves
* 2 tbsp hand-torn basil leaves

1. De-scale the fish, but do not remove the skin. Cut it open through the belly with a boning knife and remove the rib cage, but leave the bones along the backline of the fish intact, so it does not split open.

2. Combine the vinegar, lime juice, olive oil, garlic, salt and black pepper in a dish. Add the fish, toss well to coat in the marinade and refrigerate for 1 hour.

3. To make the sauce, melt the butter in a saucepan and sauté the onion, red pepper and tomato for 2 minutes over a medium heat. Stir in the fish stock, ground annatto, turmeric, parsley and culantro and simmer for 5 minutes. Season the prawns with salt and pepper, add to the pan and cook for a further 1 minute. Remove from the heat and set aside.

4. Preheat the oven to 200°C (400°F), gas mark 6.

5. To make the filling, heat the olive oil in a saucepan and sauté the chopped onion, red pepper and tomato for 2 minutes. Stir in the crab meat and prawns and cook for 3 minutes until they are almost cooked through. Add the parsley, coriander and basil, remove from the heat and reserve the prawns.

6. Spread the filling inside the fish cavity. Tie the fish with kitchen string 8 times, at regular intervals, making sure the filling is well enclosed at the seams.

7. Reserve the prawns from the sauce. Transfer the fish to a baking dish and pour the prepared sauce over it. Cover with foil and bake for 1 hour.

8. About 2 minutes before the end of cooking add the reserved prawns, stirring them back into the sauce. Return the dish to the oven until they are cooked and turn pink.

9. Discard the foil and remove the string from the fish. Use a knife to remove the backbone before serving with Brazilian-style White Rice (see page 94) and Savoury Cassava Flour Crumble (see page 86).

Pirarucu de casaca
Grilled salt fish with plantain and farofa

Pirarucu (arapaima) is a significant part of the Amazon riverside population's diet. It is usually sold as salt-cured fillets, production having been commercialized as early as the 18th century. There are three methods of salt-curing this fish: dry cure, mixed cure and brining. At Remanso do Bosque, we are continually researching food preservation, and we have developed our own method of salt-curing.

Serves 4

* 200g salted pirarucu (arapaima) or salt cod fillets
* 2 tbsp olive oil
* 1 tsp finely chopped garlic
* 1 tbsp chopped basil
* 3 tbsp chopped flat-leaf parsley
* 3 tbsp chopped coriander leaves
* 70g pitted green olives, chopped
* 50g unsalted butter
* 2 ripe plantains, peeled and sliced
* 100g grated cassava, deep-fried, to serve (optional)

Farofa
* 30ml extra virgin olive oil
* 40ml dry white wine vinegar
* 50ml unsweetened coconut milk
* salt
* 50g tomato flesh, chopped
* 70g red onion, finely sliced
* 1 tbsp chopped basil
* 3 tbsp chopped flat-leaf parsley
* 3 tbsp chopped coriander leaves
* 100g extra fine, untoasted cassava flour

1. Soak the fish in plenty of cold water for 12 hours, changing the water every 3 hours. Drain and pat dry.

2. Grill the fish until cooked, then leave to cool. Flake the flesh into pieces.

3. Heat the olive oil in a saucepan and sauté the garlic. Add the basil, parsley and coriander leaves. Stir in the fish and sauté for a few minutes. Add the olives, remove from the heat and set aside.

4. Melt the butter in a frying pan and cook the plantain until golden brown on both sides. Drain on kitchen paper and set aside.

5. To make the farofa, combine the olive oil, vinegar, coconut milk and a little salt in a mixing bowl. Whisk well, until the mixture is well combined. Add the tomato, onion, basil, parsley and coriander.

6. Gradually sprinkle the cassava flour into the bowl, stirring well to combine. When the mixture resembles moistened fresh breadcrumbs, taste and adjust the salt.

7. Preheat the oven to 160°C (325°F), gas mark 3. Arrange half the plantains in a baking dish and spread the farofa on top. Add a layer of the fish mixture and finish with the remaining plantain. Bake for 8 minutes, then remove from the oven and serve with the deep-fried cassava (if using).

Piracaia
Chargrilled fish with hot chilli sauce

Pacu fish, also known as caranha, is a freshwater fish originally found in the basins of the rivers Paraná, Paraguay and Uruguay, as well as in the Amazonian rivers, in the Pantanal and in the River Plate basin. It can reach almost 1 metre in length and 15 kilograms in weight – however, those caught today are rarely larger than 5 kilograms. Pacu is a great source of protein and healthy lipids.

Serves 4

* 4 small whole pacus or snapper, about 600g each
* 20g coarse rock salt
* 30ml lime juice
* fine, untoasted cassava flour, to serve

Bird's-eye chilli sauce
* 1 tbsp chopped pimenta malagueta (bird's-eye chilli)
* 50ml lime juice
* 1 tsp salt
* 1 tbsp chopped coriander leaves

1. To make the sauce, combine all the ingredients in a bowl, preferably one made from gourd. Add 250ml of water and stir well. Set aside.

2. Ask your fishmonger to clean the fish for you, discarding the guts and scales. The pacu's bones are interspersed in its flesh so, in the Amazon, there is a technique called ticar (literally 'tick off') that involves making cross cuts all over the body of the fish, to break the bones into smaller pieces.

3. Sprinkle the coarse salt all over the fish and drizzle it with the lime juice. Massage the fish with your hands to help the seasoning penetrate the flesh. Leave to marinate for 10 minutes.

4. Preheat a charcoal barbecue. Put the pacus in a fish grill basket and sit it 30cm above the hot coals. Chargrill for 5 minutes on each side or until cooked through. Serve with the bird's-eye sauce and cassava flour.

Tips from Thiago:
If you don't have a barbecue, use a roasting tray with a rack. Place the fish on the rack and bake in a preheated oven at 180°C (350°F), gas mark 4 for 15 minutes.

MARCELO AMARAL

Marcelo's CV reads like a spiritual journey to find his own culinary identity. He was a successful art director and left Brazil to find adventure in New Zealand, where he discovered his true passion for cooking. He moved to Australia, learned about Asian cuisine and the art of spices, and then studied Thai Royal Cuisine at the renowned Blue Elephant in Bangkok, and at the Chiang Mai Thai Cookery School.

In 2004 he opened the restaurant Lagundri in Curitiba, focusing on Asian cuisine, and received many awards as the best Asian restaurant in South Brazil. It was then that he realized he had a new mission: to find a link between Asian and Caiçara cuisine (from the coastal areas), and this became the object of his research.

Marcelo is involved in environmental projects, organic and biodynamic practices, and in the protection and rescue of caiçara dishes in the coastal cities of Antonia, Paranaguá and Morretes. He is becoming an ambassador for Caiçara cuisine in South Brazil and has found, via Asia, his true Brazilian roots.

Camarões da encosta
Prawns of the sea slope

The Caiçaras are inhabitants of coastal areas from the south of Rio de Janeiro, to the north of Paraná state. Their inheritance is an intermixing of native indigenous groups, Portuguese and Black Brazilians, and their dishes take as much advantage as possible of local products. Jackfruit was brought from India by the Portuguese, and you eat every part of it, even the seeds. Ginger came to Brazil with the slaves, and spices with the Portuguese. This recipe from Marcelo Amaral (see page 146) honours the Caiçaras and their vibrant cuisine.

Serves 4

* 500g whole raw prawns
* 10g garlic cloves, peeled
* 10g peeled root ginger
* 10g coriander roots
* 20ml canola oil
* 50g onion, finely diced
* 10g pimenta dedo-de-moça or other hot red chilli, deseeded and finely sliced
* 2 tsp dried red chilli flakes
* 300ml unsweetened coconut milk
* 3 lime leaves
* 20g rapadura or dark muscovado sugar
* 1 tbsp chopped coriander leaves, plus extra leaves to garnish
* 50g jackfruit pulp
* 1 tsp salt
* 1 tsp toasted sesame seeds

Fish stock
* 2 white fish carcasses, rinsed
* ½ celery stalk, cut into 2cm cubes
* 1 carrot, cut into 2cm cubes
* 1 onion, cut into 2cm cubes
* 30g piece of root ginger, peeled
* 1 pimenta dedo-de-moça or other hot red chilli, left whole

1. Peel the prawns, reserving the heads and shells to make the stock.

2. Ensure there is no trace of blood in the fish carcasses. Combine all the stock ingredients plus the prawn heads and shells in a saucepan with 1 litre of water. Place over a low heat and bring to simmering point. Cook for 25 minutes.

3. Strain the stock through a chinois or fine sieve and set aside.

4. Using a mortar and pestle or a bowl, pound the garlic cloves, ginger and coriander roots together to form a paste. Set aside.

5. Heat the canola oil in a wok or cast-iron frying pan over a low heat and sauté the seasoning paste for 2 minutes. Add the onion, chilli and 1 teaspoon of the dried chilli flakes. Sauté for about 4 minutes, stirring constantly to prevent burning.

6. Stir in a quarter of the coconut milk, then add the prawns and lime leaves. Gradually pour in the remaining coconut milk and 150ml of the fish stock, then add the remaining 1 teaspoon of chilli flakes, the rapadura and chopped coriander leaves.

7. Once the prawns have cooked, add the jackfruit pulp and adjust the salt to taste. Sprinkle with the extra coriander leaves and toasted sesame seeds to finish.

Tips from Marcelo:
Serve with Brazilian-style White Rice (see page 94). If you can't find jackfruit, use the same quantity of very ripe mashed banana – the Caiçara's favourite fruit!

BRAZILIANS AND MEAT

We love our meat! Grilling is an integral part of our culinary culture, particularly important in South Brazil but popular all over the country. It is equally loved whether eating at home or in churrascarias – restaurants specializing in barbecued meat, in which waiters walk around with large skewers and slice the meat onto your plate as desired.

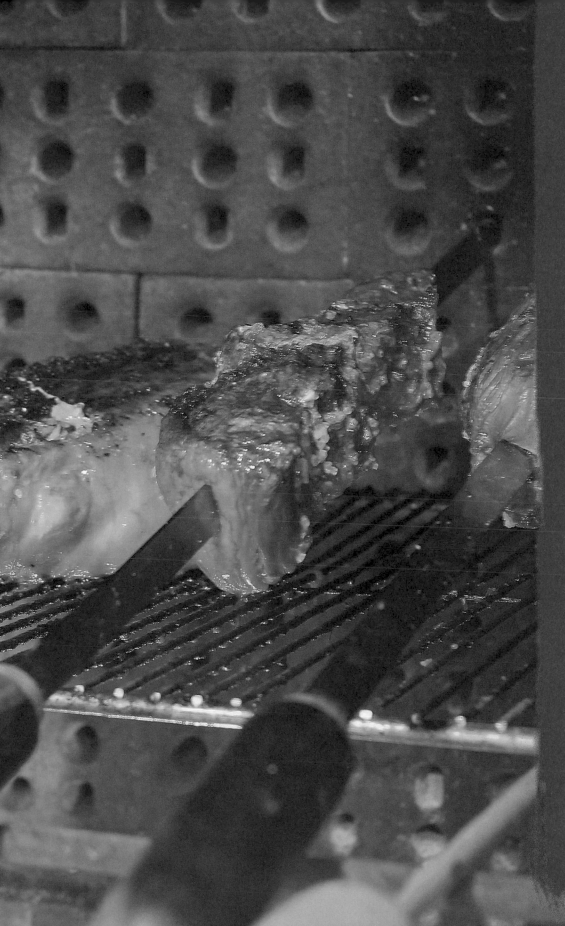

MEAT AND POULTRY FOR FIRE AND GRILL

For 15 years Júnior Durski lived and worked in the heart of the Amazonian forest running his own timber business, but his passion for food and wine resulted in a radical change of direction. In 1999 he opened a fine dining restaurant called Durski and very quickly it was hailed as one of the best restaurants in the country.

A meat specialist obsessed with quality, Júnior then set out to produce the perfect steak. He opened his first steakhouse in 2005 and, at his restaurant called Madero in Curitiba, Paraná, is now one of the most successful restaurateurs in Brazil, hoping to finish 2013 with 38 restaurants! The Madero concept includes control over ingredient production and he has built his own school for staff training. Still actively working in his main kitchen, Júnior is one of Brazil's leading experts in the art of grilling, as well as a wine expert with one of the most impressive wine cellars in the country.

PICANHA

This is a very popular cut of beef in Brazil and ideal for barbecuing. Easily distinguished by its thick layer of fat on one side, it comes from the cap, which lies above the rump areas and the top sirloin.

You will find churrascarias all over Brazil – steakhouses that serve many different cuts of meat and poultry, where you simply decide which cut you are going to eat. Serving churrasco (chargrilled meat) at home is very popular at weekends and many Brazilians have a barbecue area built in their backyards.

Arroz de carreteiro
Rice with Brazilian jerk beef, pork ribs and sausage

Arroz de carreteiro is emblematic of the Rio Grande do Sul state. Originally it consisted only of rice and carne seca, cooked together in an iron pot. Over time, each family developed their own recipe, adding to it leftover barbecued beef and other meat cuts and sausages. This is the recipe of Luiz Paulo, a gaucho who is not a chef, but makes a unique version of arroz de carreteiro.

Serves 8

* 800g carne seca, cut into 1.5cm cubes
* 120ml vegetable oil
* 500g smoked pork ribs, cut into 4cm pieces
* 150g calabresa or other smoked pork sausage, cut into 5mm slices
* 30g caster sugar
* 20g garlic, crushed
* 80g onion, diced
* 1kg short-grain white rice
* 15g spring onions, chopped
* 15g flat-leaf parsley, chopped

Tips from Luiz Paulo
Short-grain white rice is suitable for this recipe, including bomba, the Spanish paella rice and Italian arborio, carnaroli or vialone nano.

1. Rinse the beef under cold running water. Put it in a large saucepan, add cold water to cover and cook over a very low heat for about 20 minutes.

2. Drain the water, add more cold water to cover and cook for a further 20 minutes. Repeat the procedure at least twice more. Taste the meat for saltiness and, if necessary, repeat once more.

3. Heat the oil in a cast-iron saucepan and brown the prepared carne seca, pork ribs and sausage. Remove the meat from the pan and set aside.

4. Add the sugar to the same pan and cook until melted and caramelized. Return the meat to the pan, add the garlic and onion and sauté until they begin to colour. Add the rice and sauté, stirring carefully until the grains are slightly golden brown.

5. Add about 1.5 litres or just enough boiling water to cover the ingredients. Cover and cook over a medium heat until the meat is cooked through and the rice is tender but still firm to the bite. Stir occasionally to prevent the rice sticking to the bottom of the pan. Add more boiling water if needed. Serve hot, scattered with spring onions and parsley.

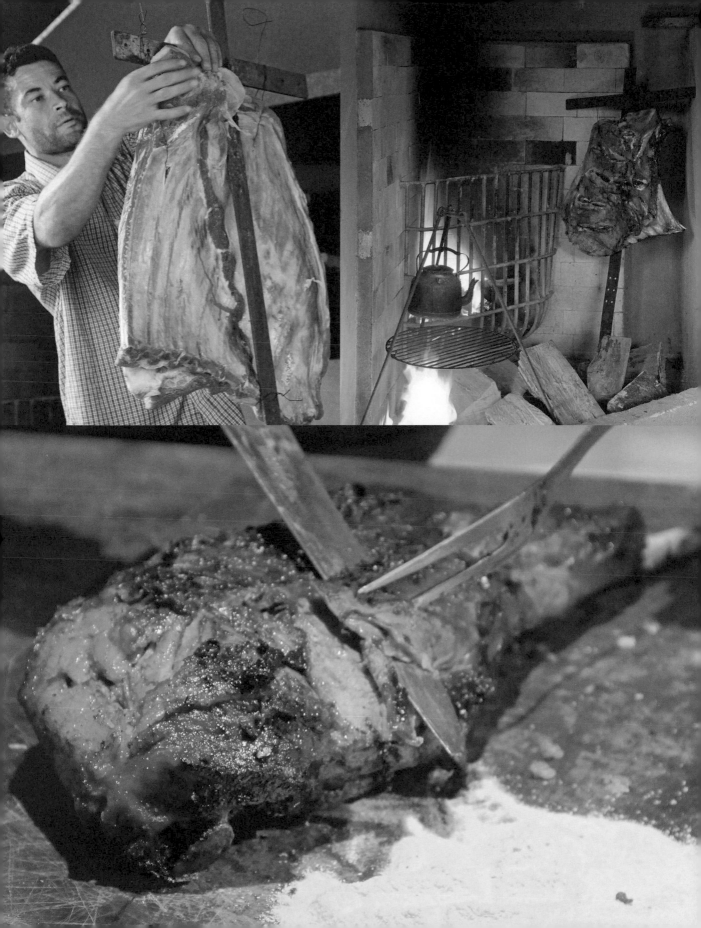

Barreado da Lindamara
Lindamara's slow-cooked stew

The name barreado (barro means clay) comes from the fact that the pot and its lid are sealed by a 'clay' made of water and flour. Opinions are divided about the origins of this dish; some suggest that Tupi-Guarani native Indians created the recipe, others give credit to the Azores in Portugal. Antonina, Morretes and Paranaguá are the three cities in which barreado is a cultural attraction, each with their own version of the recipe. This recipe, given to me by Marcelo Amaral (see page 146), is from Lindamara, a resident of Antonina, who has turned her home into a restaurant serving barreado. She cooks it in a typical Caiçara brick oven using a recipe that has been in her family for three generations. The secret, she says, is low and slow cooking for 20–30 hours.

Serves 10

Beef stock
* 2kg thick rib bones
* 200g onion, cubed
* 200g leeks, cubed
* 200g carrots, cubed
* 200g celery, cubed

Barreado
* 350g slab bacon, cut into 5mm cubes
* 20g garlic, crushed
* 400g onion, finely diced
* 5kg beef brisket or topside, cut into 3cm cubes
* 6 bay leaves
* 20g ground cumin
* 4g ground black pepper
* 3g dried red chilli flakes
* 5 tbsp plain flour
* salt

To serve
* about 1.5kg fine, untoasted cassava flour
* 5 bananas, peeled and sliced
* 4 oranges, peeled and sliced

1. To make the beef stock, preheat the oven to 150°C (300°F), gas mark 2. Put the bones and vegetables in a roasting tray and roast for about 1 hour or until golden brown.

2. Tip the roasted ingredients and any cooking juices into a large saucepan. Add 3 litres of water and simmer over a medium heat until the volume of liquid has reduced by a third. Strain the stock through muslin and set aside.

3. In a large clay pot with a well-fitting lid, arrange the barreado ingredients in layers, starting with half the bacon, then the garlic, onion, and half the beef. Add the other half of the bacon and beef, then finish with the bay leaves, cumin, black pepper and chilli flakes.

4. Pour in about 2 litres or enough beef stock to cover the ingredients by about 10cm.

5. Put the flour in a small bowl and add enough water to make a sticky glue-like dough. Cover the clay pot with its lid and use the dough to seal the container and keep the steam inside.

6. Simmer over the lowest possible heat for 20–30 hours. At the end of cooking, break off the dough seal. Taste the stew and adjust the salt as needed. Serve with plenty of cassava flour and the sliced bananas and oranges.

Tips from Marcelo:
Serve with lots of broth in a wide bowl. Let each diner add the cassava flour to the broth little by little, stirring with a fork, until the mixture has a porridge-like consistency. Brazilian-style White Rice (see page 94), and Pickled Kiss Peppers (see page 103) are the ideal accompaniment.

Feijoada completa
Brazilian black bean and meat stew

Feijoada, a hearty combination of beans and meat similar to a French cassoulet, first became famous in the kitchens of Rio de Janeiro, but it is now loved throughout Brazil. Associated with relaxing in the company of family and friends, it is typically served on Sundays, alongside caipirinhas (see page 38) and cold beer. This is the award-winning version prepared at the well-known Bar da Dona Onça, in São Paulo (see page 22).

Serves 10

* 1kg dried black beans, rinsed and sorted
* 300g carne de sol or carne seca
* 2 whole oranges, rinsed
* 10 cloves
* 10 bay leaves
* 100g pig's ear
* 150g pig's tail
* 200g pig's trotter
* 200g pancetta, chopped
* 150g paio sausage or other thick, mild smoked pork sausage
* 300g beef shoulder clod
* 150g Portuguese linguiça sausage
* 200g beef tongue
* 80ml cachaça
* 1 tbsp lard
* 200g slab bacon, chopped
* 300g onion, diced
* 100g garlic, crushed
* salt

1. Soak the beans in cold water for at least 6 hours or overnight. At the same time, soak the carne de sol or carne seca, changing the water every hour (five times is enough).

2. When ready to cook, drain the beans and beef. Stud the oranges with the cloves and tie the bay leaves in a bundle.

3. In a very large pot, combine the beans, oranges and bay; then arrange the meat on top of the beans in this order: pig's ear, tail and trotter, carne de sol, pancetta, paio sausage, beef shoulder, whole sausages and the beef tongue. Pour in the cachaça and add enough water to cover.

4. Bring the water to the boil and skim off the foam that rises to the surface.

5. When the sausages begin to take on the colour of the black beans, remove them from the pan and set aside. Cook for a further 15 minutes, then start testing the meats to see if they are ready by poking them with a long-handled fork. As they become tender, lift them from the pan and set aside, always following the inverse order in which they were added to the pot. When you get down to the carne de sol the beans should be cooked. Continue taking the cooked meats out of the pan until they are all done. This procedure should take no more than 2½ hours.

6. Skim any remaining foam from the surface and discard the orange and bundle of bay leaves. Peel the beef tongue and slice it into thin slices. Cut all the other meats into 3cm cubes and the sausages into 1.5cm rounds.

7. Heat the lard in a frying pan. Add the bacon, onion and garlic and a little salt. Sauté the mixture until golden brown, then stir it into the pot to season the beans.

8. Return all the meat to the pot and let the feijoada simmer until all the flavours have mingled and the broth has thickened. Serve with the traditional accompaniments (see tips, opposite).

Tips from Janaina and Jefferson:
The traditional feijoada is served with Brazilian-style White Rice (see page 94), Savoury Cassava Flour Crumble (see page 86), stir-fried flat-leaf kale, tomato and onion salsa, and orange slices. Creative cooks always come up with slightly different combinations – white rice is essential, but if you are feeling adventurous, just aim to serve the stew with some kind of farofa, a stir-fried leafy green and a sweet and sour element. The meats given here can be substituted with other parts of the pig that you prefer, but don't forget to include selected smoked cuts and sausages.

Thirty-one year old Felipe Rameh has worked at some of the best restaurants in the world, including Alex Atala's D.O.M., Andoni Luiz Aduriz's Mugaritz, and has worked with the father of Brazilian cuisine Paulo Martins learning the secrets of native Brazilian ingredients. Now a rising star in Brazil, at Restaurant Trindade in Belo Horizonte, Minas Gerais, Felipe's innovative dishes have their own identity and focus on local and iconic products from his region.

Felipe and his business partner (and fellow chef) Fred Trindade work closely with the artist Rogério Fernandes and also with local producers and coffee specialists (see page 244). Felipe is knowledgeable about new technology and modern techniques, and his cuisine celebrates the evolution of classic dishes. Trindade is a very authentic restaurant – a reference point in Brazil for excellence and creativity.

Jarrete de porco, café e rapadura
Pig's trotters, coffee and rapadura

This dish raises the status of one of the less noble parts of the pig while celebrating the most loved product of Brazil – coffee! Brazil is the world's top producer and exporter of coffee with Minas Gerais the main growing region holding about 50 per cent of the Brazilian crop. At Trindade, Felipe (see page 166) uses the products of Academia do Café, headed by Bruno Souza – an expert in Brazilian coffee, who supports small producers (see page 244).

Serves 2

* 2 pig's trotters
* sea salt flakes and black pepper
* ¼ tsp finely chopped rosemary
* 2–3 garlic cloves, crushed
* zest of ½ rangpur (mandarin lime)
* 1 tsp rangpur (mandarin lime) juice
* 20g rapadura or dark muscovado sugar
* 30g roasted coffee beans
* 20g butter
* 20ml olive oil

Pork demi-glace

* 4kg pork bones (foot, hock, trotters) and/or beef bones
* 600g cow's foot
* 2 onions
* 2 carrots
* ½ small celery stalk
* ½ small leek
* 2 tbsp rapeseed oil
* 25g coriander seeds
* 500ml dry red wine
* 250ml Madeira wine
* 2 tomatoes
* 1 bouquet garni made with 2 thyme sprigs, 1 rosemary sprig and 2 bay leaves

1. To make the demi-glace, preheat the oven to 180°C (350°F), gas mark 4. Put the bones and cow's foot in a roasting tin and roast for 1 hour or until light golden brown. If you roast them for too long the demi-glace will be bitter.

2. Chop the onions, carrots, celery and leek into 5cm chunks. Heat the oil in a large pot and sauté the onions until lightly coloured. Add the carrot, celery, leek and half the coriander seeds and sauté until golden brown.

3. Transfer the roasted bones to the pot. Pour in half the red wine and half the Madeira. Add the tomatoes, bouquet garni and enough cold water to completely cover the ingredients. Simmer over a very low heat for about 40 hours (you can stop the cooking overnight and restart the next morning to complete the 40 hours). Halfway through cooking, add another 2.5 litres of water.

4. Strain the mixture into a clean pot, discarding the solids. Add the remaining red wine and madeira. Lightly toast the remaining coriander seeds in a clean, dry frying pan and add to the pot. Simmer, uncovered, until the liquid has reduced to about 1 litre. Strain again, leave to cool and then chill the demi-glace.

5. Rinse the trotters, pat dry with kitchen paper and season with the rosemary, garlic, the zest and juice of the rangpur and some salt and black pepper. Leave to marinate for 4 hours.

6. Heat the butter and the olive oil in a large, heavy-based, cast-iron frying pan and brown the trotters on all sides, then set aside.

7. Preheat the oven to 220°C (425°F), gas mark 7. Transfer the pig's trotters to a roasting tin and roast for about 30 minutes or until dark golden brown. Cover with foil, lower the oven temperature to 170°C (340°F), gas mark 3½, and continue roasting until the meat starts to fall off the bone. Check the meat after 2 hours – the amount of time needed will depend on the size of the trotters.

8. Discard the layer of fat that has accumulated on top of the chilled demi-glace. In a small saucepan, heat 200ml of the demi-glace, stir in the rapadura until dissolved, then add the coffee beans. Turn off the heat and leave to infuse for 1 hour, then strain.

9. Reheat the sauce and serve it drizzled over the hot pig's trotters.

Lombinho defumado, palmito do cerrado e doce de leite

Smoked pork tenderloin, hearts of palm and milk caramel sauce

This recipe from Felipe Rameh (see page 166) features some of the key ingredients of Minas Gerais cuisine: pork, cachaça and milk caramel. Hearts of palm, much loved by Brazilians, can be extracted from various palm trees, but more than 90 per cent of the production comes from three types of tree: the açaí, the juçara and peach palm trees. Always buy from sustainable sources.

Serves 2

* 500g pork tenderloin
* salt and white pepper
* 300g wood chips, preferably cachaça cask chips such as umburana
* 100g dry wood sticks
* 10g clarified butter or ghee
* 15g butter
* nasturtium leaves, to decorate (optional)

Hearts of palm

* 1 whole heart of palm, in the husk, about 1kg, or ready-cooked hearts of palm from a jar
* 20g pork lard
* 10g butter
* sea salt flakes

Milk caramel sauce

* 250ml Pork Demi-glace (see page 169)
* 60g low-sugar dulce de leche
* chopped hot chillies preserved in oil

1. Trim the pork and season with salt and white pepper. Wrap in cling film and twist the ends to form a log shape. Preheat the oven to 110°C (225°F), gas mark ¼.

2. Place the wood chips and sticks in a roasting tin and cover with a wire rack ready to smoke the meat as soon as it comes out of the oven. Also have ready some foil and something to light the wood.

3. Heat the clarified butter in a cast-iron or flameproof frying pan until very hot. Unwrap the pork and sear the meat on all sides until golden brown. Add the butter to the pan and turn the meat to coat it in the butter as it melts. Transfer the pork to the oven and roast for 8 minutes.

4. Remove the meat from the oven. Light the wood chips and place the tenderloin on the wire rack. Cover the tray with foil and smoke for 10 seconds. Carve the tenderloin in slices and set aside.

5. (Omit this step if using ready-cooked hearts of palm from a jar and continue the recipe from step 8). To cook the heart of palm, reduce the oven temperature to 90°C (195°F), gas mark < ¼. Wrap the palm in foil and bake for 1 hour 20 minutes or until tender but firm.

6. Remove the palm from the oven and discard the foil. Cut the palm into three equal rounds and then cut each in half lengthways.

7. Heat the lard and butter in a cast-iron frying pan and fry the hearts of palm until dark and golden. Season with flaky sea salt.

8. To make the sauce, heat the demi-glace in a shallow frying pan, then add the dulce de leche and chillies and cook for 3 minutes. Remove the pan from the heat and leave the chilli to infuse for 10 minutes before straining.

9. On each serving plate, alternate the hearts of palm with the sliced pork. Drizzle with a little milk caramel sauce and finish with a sprinkle of flaky sea salt and a few nasturtium leaves for decoration.

Carne de sereno da dona Azely
Mrs Azely's salt-cured beef

This is a traditional family dish, created by Fred Trindade's grandmother Dona Azely (see page 166). In Portuguese carne de sereno means 'dew meat', so it is ideally made overnight. The pequi, a fruit native to the Brazilian Cerrado (tropical savannah), is much loved in the cuisine of Minas Gerais and its intense aroma is unmistakable.

Serves 12

* 300g salt, plus extra for seasoning
* 3kg boneless piece Angus beef topside or sirloin
* 12 fresh pequis (see tip, below)
* 1 onion, chopped
* 3 garlic cloves, chopped
* 15 coriander seeds
* 2 red bird's-eye chillies, chopped
* 50g ground annatto (achiote)
* 2kg shelled fresh feijão-andu or other fresh beans
* 150ml manteiga de garrafa or clarified butter or ghee (see tip on page 76)
* 800g untoasted white cassava flour, preferably Morro Alto
* 50g flat-leaf parsley, chopped
* 20g spring onions, chopped

1. Rub the 300g of salt all over the meat, packing it firmly on the surface. Use a meat hook to hang the meat in a cool, dry place away from any insects and leave it to cure overnight. Before use, remove the excess salt by rinsing the meat thoroughly under cold running water.

2. Put the pequis in a saucepan of salted water. Bring to the boil and cook for about 50 minutes. Turn off the heat and keep the pequis in the water to keep them hot.

3. Meanwhile, put the onion, garlic, coriander seeds, chilli, annatto and 50g of salt in a large wooden mortar. Pound vigorously with a pestle to form a smooth paste.

4. Bring a saucepan of salted water to the boil. Add the beans and cook until soft but not mushy. Drain and set aside.

5. Heat 100ml of the manteiga de garrafa in a heavy-based saucepan and sauté the seasoning paste. Add the cooked beans and cassava flour and stir to combine. Add the parsley and spring onions. Remove from the heat and set aside.

6. Cut the meat against the grain into 3cm-thick steaks. Heat a cast-iron frying pan, add the remaining 50ml of the manteiga de garrafa and cook the steaks for about 1 minute on each side for rare meat, longer if you prefer medium-rare or well done.

7. Serve the cooked pequis and the fresh bean farofa in saucepans and the steaks on a wooden cutting board.

Tips from Fred:
If you cannot hang the meat in a safe place, wrap it in cling film and refrigerate for 24 hours, turning the meat once or twice during curing. If fresh pequis are not available, look for brined pequis, whole or slivered, or pequi paste or oil; they are available in Brazilian stores and online. Each of these products is ready to use, and each person can add as much as they want.

RODRIGO OLIVEIRA

Mocotó is the most authentic Brazilian restaurant in São Paulo, the gastronomic capital of Brazil. It began in the 1970s with José Oliveira de Almeida, Rodrigo's father, who came from the backland of Pernambuco state to open a small business with his brothers. He sold bone marrow soup and became successful when people began to queue for a bowl of the delicacy. At 13 years old Rodrigo was already helping his father, but Seu José wanted to see his son going to university, not the kitchen! Rodrigo began his studies in environmental engineering, but decided after a while to change to a gastronomy degree.

With new ideas, great talent, and a humble attitude, he turned a small bar into a new culinary concept where traditional food and modern techniques are partners. Democratic cuisine is the motto at Mocotó – no reservations, affordable prices and comfort food without fuss.

Mocotó also serves an impressive selection of artisan cachaças, and 'dangerously delicious' cocktails (see the caipirinha recipes on page 38).

Rodrigo Oliveira

Mocofava
Cow's foot and broad bean stew

People wait in long queues just to have a bowl of this stew of cow's foot (mocotó) and broad beans (fava) called mocofava, the most famous dish of the Mocotó restaurant (see page 174). A single spoon of hot mocofava can transport you immediately to the backlands of Brazil: 100 per cent comfort food.

Serves 12

* 500g dried broad beans, rinsed and sorted
* 300g charque, cut into cubes
* ½ cow's foot, cut into pieces (see tip)
* 1 small onion, chopped
* 2 small tomatoes, chopped
* ½ yellow or red pepper, chopped
* 5 garlic cloves
* ½ tbsp ground cumin
* ½ tbsp colorau, ground annatto or achiote
* ½ tsp ground coriander
* ½ tsp ground white pepper
* 150g smoked slab bacon, rind removed, cubed
* 150g smoked pork sausage, sliced
* 2 small bay leaves
* 1 fresh mandarin lime (rangpur) leaf or regular lime leaf or kaffir lime leaf
* 25g lard
* 75g streaky bacon, diced
* 25g manteiga de garrafa or clarified butter or ghee (see tip on page 76)
* chopped flat-leaf parsley, spring onions and coriander leaves, to taste
* salt

1. Soak the beans in cold water overnight. At the same time, soak the charque in a separate bowl, changing the water five times at hourly intervals to remove the excess salt. Then, in a pan of fresh water, cook the charque until it is fork tender (about 1½ hours).

2. Cook the cow's foot in plenty of fresh water for 60 minutes in a pressure cooker (or 6 hours on the stove) until tender. Remove the cow's foot from the pot and, when cool enough to handle, discard the bones, cartilage and rind. Cut up the meat and set aside. Drain the beans and cook in fresh water for 35 minutes or until tender.

3. Combine the onion, tomatoes, yellow or red pepper, garlic, cumin, colorau, ground coriander and white pepper in a blender or food processor and process to a smooth paste.

4. Put the paste in a large pot and add the cooked charque, smoked slab bacon, sliced sausage, bay leaves, lime leaf and the broad beans with their cooking liquid. Add more water, if needed. Cook for about 20 minutes or until the broth has thickened.

5. Heat the lard in a frying pan and fry the diced bacon. Add this to the pot together with the reserved cow's foot and the manteiga de garrafa. Leave the stew to cook for a further 10 minutes. Add the chopped parsley, spring onions and coriander to taste, then check whether it needs any salt (see tip, below). Serve hot, with toasted cassava flour and hot pepper sauce on the side.

Tips from Rodrigo:
Whether you need extra salt will depend partly on how many times you have changed the water when soaking the charque. Ask your butcher to split the cow's foot in half lengthways and to cut it into smaller chunks – this will make your life easier.

Carne de sol do Mocotó
Mocotó's Brazilian-style jerk beef

Carne de sol is very popular in the northeast region of the country. At Mocotó (see page 174), it is served with cassava crisps.

Serves 8

* 2kg beef topside or sirloin roast
* about 60g coarse rock salt
* 100g manteiga de garrafa or clarified butter or ghee
* vegetable oil, for deep-frying
* 300g cassava root, peeled

To serve
* 8 garlic bulbs
* sea salt
* 1 tsp dried thyme
* 1 tsp dried oregano
* olive oil, for drizzling
* jar of pimenta biquinho (kiss peppers)

1. Trim the meat and cut along the grain into two long strips. Rub the salt all over the surface. For thicker pieces of meat you will need a little more salt; for thinner pieces, a little less. Refrigerate for 24 hours, turning the meat three times during this period.

2. Hang the meat overnight in a cool, dry place, away from any insects.

3. Next day, scrape the excess salt from the meat. Vacuum seal it in a sous-vide bag with half of the manteiga de garrafa and cook sous-vide for 18 hours at 63°C. Alternatively, you can confit the meat following the instructions in the tip below. Let the beef cool, saving any juices.

4. To prepare the roast garlic accompaniment, slice the tops off the garlic bulbs and place in a roasting dish. Sprinkle with salt, the dried thyme and oregano, and drizzle with olive oil. Cover the dish with aluminium foil and bake in a preheated oven at 180°C (350°F), gas mark 4, for 1½ hours or until soft and cooked through.

5. In a deep-fat fryer or heavy-based saucepan, preheat the oil to 180°C. Slice the cassava thinly using a mandoline. Deep-fry the cassava slices, in batches if necessary, until golden brown, then remove and drain on kitchen paper.

6. Heat the remaining manteiga de garrafa in a large frying pan and brown the meat on all sides. Deglaze the pan with the reserved beef juices to moisten the meat and add the peppers to the pan to heat through. Slice the meat and serve immediately with the roasted garlic, peppers and cassava crisps.

Tips from Rodrigo:
If you don't have the equipment to cook sous-vide, use the traditional confit method instead. Cover the beef with equal portions of melted pork lard and clarified butter and cook over a very low heat (70–82°C) for about 4 hours.

PAI E FILHO } FATHER AND SON

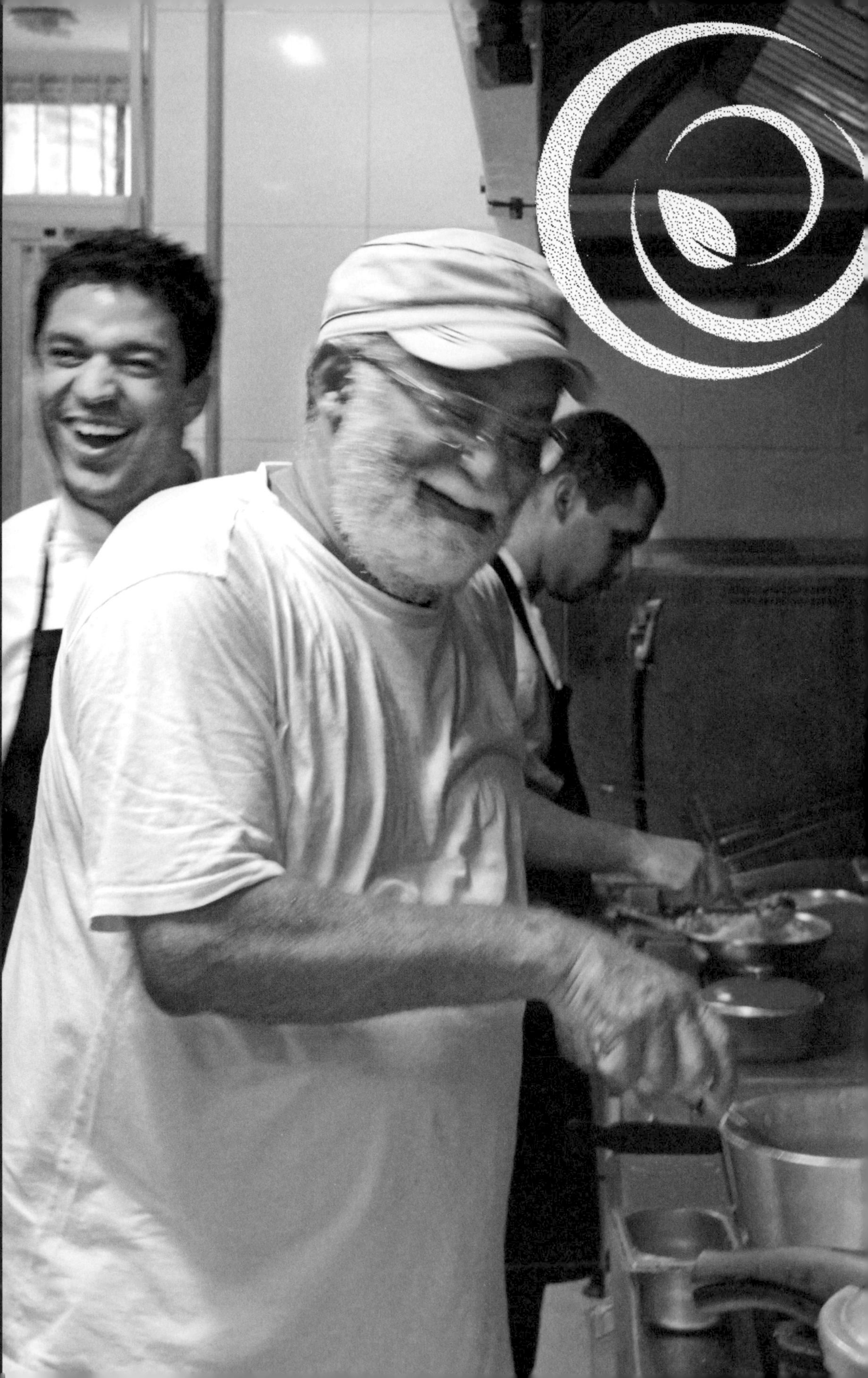

Picado de filé

Buffalo tenderloin with fried quail egg and shoestring cassava

This trio of beef, rice and egg represents the Brazilian worker's lunch, be it a workman who takes his packed lunch to a building site or an office clerk eating a meal at a restaurant. It is also the everyday lunch of many Brazilians at home, usually complemented by a simple tomato and lettuce salad with lime vinaigrette. The beef can also be served as a thin steak, sautéed with sliced onions and accompanied by stewed beans and farofa, but in our restaurant we prepare this dish with buffalo tenderloin.

Serves 2

* 400g buffalo tenderloin, cubed
* salt and black pepper
* 2 tbsp rapeseed or palm oil
* 1 tbsp butter
* 50g onion, chopped
* 100ml stout
* 1 tbsp chopped flat-leaf parsley
* 2 quail eggs or small hen eggs

Cassava fries
* vegetable oil, for deep-frying
* 300g cassava root, peeled
* sea salt flakes

Tips from Thiago:
You can substitute beef fillet for the buffalo, following the same recipe. As well as the cassava fries, Brazilian-style White Rice (see page 94) and Savoury Cassava Flour Crumble with Banana (see page 86) are perfect side dishes for this dish.

1. Season the tenderloin with salt and pepper. Heat a large frying pan until very hot. Add a drizzle of oil and arrange the meat cubes so they do not touch each other. Sear for 1 minute on each side, then remove from the pan and set aside.

2. Melt the butter in the same pan and sauté the onion until softened. Add the stout and parsley and simmer until the liquid has reduced by half. Return the meat to the pan, cook for a further 1 minute then remove from the heat and keep warm. Adjust the salt to taste.

3. To make the fries: In a deep-fat fryer or heavy-based saucepan, preheat the oil to 180°C. Cut the cassava lengthways into fine, rectangular slices, then pile a few slices together and cut the slices crossways into fine sticks. Soak them in cold water for 1 minute, then drain well and pat dry.

4. Deep-fry the cassava sticks, in batches if necessary, until golden brown, then remove, drain on kitchen paper and sprinkle with flaky sea salt.

5. In a small frying pan, heat the remaining canola oil over a low heat. Fry the quail eggs for 1½ minutes, until the white is set and the yolk runny. Transfer to warmed plates and serve with the tenderloin and cassava fries.

Vaca atolada
Braised beef ribs with cassava root

Southerners contend that this recipe originated in the south of Brazil, with the drovers who would preserve beef in its fat for their trips. On their way, they would forage for cassava roots and herbs and add them to the meat. People from Minas Gerais, however, say that this recipe is rooted in their region, in the rural area. Disagreements aside, it is a much-loved dish throughout Brazil and, although there are several versions of the recipe, two main ingredients are always present: beef ribs and cassava. This is my version, with a Pará-ish touch.

Serves 4

* 2kg beef ribs, cut into 3cm x 2cm chunks
* 30ml extra virgin olive oil
* 80g onion, finely chopped
* 60g carrot, cubed
* 80g tomato, chopped
* 1 tbsp crushed garlic
* 1 tbsp chopped pimenta-de-cheiro or other mild chilli
* 1 tbsp ground annatto (achiote)
* 2 bay leaves
* 2 tbsp chopped culantro (Mexican/ long coriander)
* 500g cassava roots, peeled and chopped into 6 x 2.5cm pieces
* salt
* 400g jambu (Pará cress/toothache plant), tender leaves and fine stems only, or spinach or watercress
* 2 tbsp chopped flat-leaf parsley

Marinade

* 60g onion, roughly chopped
* 1 tbsp crushed garlic
* ½ tsp ground black pepper
* ½ tsp ground cumin
* 200ml stout

1. Start with the marinade. Put all the ingredients in a blender, add 1 tablespoon of salt and process to a paste. Put the ribs in a non-reactive dish and pour the marinade over them. Cover and leave to marinate in the refrigerator for 2 hours.

2. Heat the olive oil in a pot and sauté the onion, carrot, tomato, garlic, pimenta-de-cheiro and annatto until golden brown. Add the marinated ribs and cook over a medium heat for about 10 minutes, stirring occasionally, until browned.

3. Add the bay leaves and culantro. Lower the heat, cover the pan and braise for 2 hours, stirring every 15 minutes. As the liquid starts to dry out, add a little water, but only enough to keep the meat moist.

4. Meanwhile put 2 litres of water and 2 tablespoons of salt in a separate saucepan. Add the cassava roots and simmer for 20 minutes until they are fork tender. Remove from the heat, drain and set aside.

5. After 2 hours of braising, add the cooked cassava, jambu and parsley to the pot of ribs and cook for a final 5 minutes. Serve at once.

Pato no tucupi com jambu
Duck in cassava juice sauce with Pará cress

Carnes e aves para o fogo e a grelha } Meat and poultry for fire and grill

This is the most traditional dish of Brazil's North and, like Maniçoba (see page 46), is associated with the religious festivities of Círio de Nazaré. However it is enjoyed throughout the year by the families of Pará and traditionally prepared using wild ducks, which have darker meat and a fuller flavour.

Serves 6

* 1 wild duck, about 2.5kg, jointed, or goose
* 3 tsp lime juice
* 3 tsp coarse rock salt
* 7 garlic cloves, finely chopped
* 120g onion, cubed
* ½ tsp ground black pepper
* ½ tsp cumin seeds
* 100ml white wine
* 20g fine salt
* 30ml extra virgin olive oil
* 5 pimentas-de-cheiro or other mild chillies, crushed
* 2 litres Tucupi substitute (see page 104)
* 3 tbsp hand-torn culantro (Mexican/long coriander)
* 3 tbsp hand-torn basil
* 3 bay leaves
* handful of jambu (Pará cress/toothache plant) or watercress or spinach

1. Put the duck pieces in a baking dish, season with the coarse salt and lime juice and leave to stand for 5 minutes.

2. Bring 3 litres of water to the boil, then pour over the duck to scald it and leave to soak for 3 minutes. Drain, then immediately plunge the duck pieces into a bowl of iced water. Drain and transfer to a roasting tin.

3. In a blender or food processor, combine 1 teaspoon of the finely chopped garlic, 60g of the onion, the pepper, cumin, white wine and fine salt. Blend to a smooth paste.

4. Cover the duck pieces with the spice paste, cover and leave to marinate in the refrigerator for 4 hours.

5. Heat the olive oil in a large saucepan and sauté the remaining onion and garlic and the pimentas-de-cheiro until softened.

6. Wipe the excess paste from the duck pieces. Add the duck to the pan. Reduce the heat to very low. Add a little water and braise for 1 hour, gradually adding up to 300ml of water to keep the pan moist. The cooking time will vary according to the type of duck used.

7. Once the duck is tender, transfer it to a roasting tray, reserving the liquid in the pan. Add the tucupi, culantro, basil and bay leaves to the braising liquid and cook for 5 minutes.

8. Preheat the oven to 200°C (400°F), gas mark 6, and roast the duck pieces, skin-side up, for 10–15 minutes or until golden brown.

9. Bring a little salted water to the boil in a saucepan, add the jambu leaves and cook for a few seconds. Drain, then plunge them immediately into a bowl of iced water. Drain and set aside.

10. Return the roasted duck to the sauce and bring to a simmer. Lower the heat, add the blanched jambu and cook for 8 minutes before serving hot with Brazilian-style White Rice (see page 94).

Tips from Thiago:
If you have any left over, use it to make the Risotto with Duck, Cassava Broth and Pará Cress on the following page.

Miniarroz com pato, tucupi e jambu
Risotto with duck, cassava broth and Pará cress

This is a variation on the Duck in Cassava Juice Sauce (see previous page) using the leftovers. Most people use long-grain rice to prepare the pilaf, but my version uses mini arroz (literally mini rice) – an all-Brazilian grain of unmatched quality.

Serves 6

* about 1.5kg of leftover boneless duck meat
  from the Duck in Cassava Juice Sauce recipe (see previous page)
* 50ml olive oil, plus a little extra for drizzling
* 50g chopped onion
* 10g minced garlic
* 30g chopped red pepper
* 5g chopped pimenta-de-cheiro or other mild chilli
* 400g mini arroz or bomba (paella) rice
* 1 litre of the leftover tucupi broth from the Duck in Cassava
  Juice Sauce recipe (see previous page), warmed
* 2 tbsp hand-torn culantro (Mexican/long coriander)
* 2 tbsp chopped sweet basil
* 2 tbsp chopped coriander leaves
* 400g jambu or Pará cress or watercress, coarsely chopped
  (discard thicker stems only)
* 2 tbsp chopped flat-leaf parsley
* 30g chopped Brazil nuts

1. Tear the duck meat into bite-sized pieces and set aside.

2. Heat the olive oil in a large saucepan and sauté the onion, garlic, red pepper and pimenta-de-cheiro until wilted.

3. Add the rice and duck to the pan and sauté for 1 minute.

4. Stir in the hot tucupi broth, culantro, sweet basil and coriander. Cover the pan and simmer over a very low heat, stirring occasionally, for about 18 minutes or until the rice is tender, but firm to the bite.

5. About 2 minutes before turning off the heat, add the jambu to the pan and toss to combine.

6. Turn off the heat, stir in the parsley and Brazil nuts and finish with a drizzle of olive oil. Cover and leave to stand for 2 minutes before serving.

Galinha caipira
Braised chicken

For my father, Seu Chicão (see page 136), this dish, my grandmother's recipe, represents the comfort of rural family homes. My brother Felipe and I grew up eating this at our grandma's house. It is simple and easy to make, but needs care and the best ingredients. Choose an organic chicken from a free-range source.

Serves 2–3

* 1 whole free-range chicken
* 1½ tbsp finely chopped onion
* 1 tbsp chopped garlic, plus 1 tbsp crushed garlic
* 1 tsp ground cumin
* salt
* 2 bay leaves
* 3 large potatoes, peeled and chopped into 5cm rounds
* 3 carrots, peeled and chopped into 5cm rounds
* 30ml olive oil
* 15ml annatto (achiote) oil
* 40g chopped red onion
* 2 tbsp each chopped red, green and yellow peppers
* 2 tbsp coriander leaves
* 3 tbsp chopped culantro (Mexican/long coriander)

1. Cut the chicken into joints, then cut each joint (including the breasts) in half. Crush the onion, chopped garlic and cumin together with a little salt to form a paste. Tear up the bay leaves by hand and mix them into the paste. Rub this mixture over the chicken and leave to marinate for 1 hour.

2. Put the potatoes and carrots in a saucepan of salted water, bring to the boil and cook for 10 minutes or until they are cooked, but still firm to the bite. Drain and set aside.

3. In a large saucepan, heat the olive and annatto oils together and sauté the onion, the red, green and yellow peppers, the crushed garlic, coriander leaves and culantro for 2 minutes.

4. Wipe the excess marinade from the chicken pieces, then add the chicken to the pan. Sauté for about 10 minutes.

5. Add 1.5 litres of water and some salt to taste. Cook for 40 minutes, turning the chicken pieces every now and then, until they are cooked through. If needed, add more water to prevent the sauce drying out.

6. Add the carrot and potato to the pan and cook for a further 1 minute. When ready, the sauce should come about halfway up the sides of the pan. Serve with Brazilian-style White Rice (see page 94).

Cozido de feijão-manteiguinha com carne moqueada na folha de guarimã

Bean stew with leaf-wrapped chargrilled meat

I learned this recipe from one of our cooks, Heiliedro Tavares. He is passionate about food, has a well-trained palate and always has a lot to teach us. Moquém is an indigenous preservation process that involves chargrilling ingredients at a very low heat for long periods of time until they dry. However, in this recipe we place the meat closer to the heat source for a shorter time, to avoid overcooking.

Serves 8

* 2 salted pig's trotters
* 100g carne seca, cut into large cubes
* 500g dried feijão-manteiguinha or black-eyed beans
* 600g beef topside, rump or sirloin, in one piece
* 2 tbsp coarse rock salt
* 30ml extra virgin olive oil
* 100g slab bacon, cut into large cubes
* 50g onion, diced
* 1 tbsp chopped garlic
* 60g paio or other smoked pork sausage, cut into thick slices
* 2 bay leaves
* ½ tsp ground cumin
* salt and black pepper
* 100g winter squash or pumpkin, deseeded and cut into large cubes
* 2 guarimã leaves or banana leaves
* 3 tbsp chopped culantro (Mexican/long coriander)
* 3 tbsp chopped basil

1. Soak the pig's trotters and carne seca in cold water for 12 hours, changing the water every 3 hours to remove excess salt. At the same time in a separate bowl, soak the beans in cold water.

2. Drain the carne seca and pig's trotters, then put them in a pot and cover with fresh water. Bring to simmering point and cook the carne seca for 30 minutes and the pig's trotters for 1 hour, or until tender. Set aside in the cooking liquid.

3. Sprinkle the surface of the beef topside with the coarse salt and leave in the refrigerator to 'bleed' for 3 hours.

4. In a heavy-based pot, heat the olive oil and sauté the bacon, onion and garlic until light golden brown. Add the paio, bay leaves, cumin and some black pepper.

5. Drain the beans and add them to the onion mixture in the pot. Pour in enough cold water to cover. Put the lid on and simmer for 40 minutes or until the beans are tender. If needed, add more water a little at a time to the pot during cooking.

6. Add the carne seca and pig's trotters, plus their cooking liquid, to the pot of beans. Follow with the squash and cook for a further 20 minutes. If you prefer a stew with more sauce, add extra water as required.

7. Preheat a charcoal barbecue. Wrap the beef topside in the guarimã leaves and sit it 40cm above the hot coals. Cook for 8 minutes on each side, until the leaf is charred and the meat is just pink in the centre.

8. Sprinkle the culantro and basil over the hot bean stew and serve with the leaf-wrapped beef.

Chibé
Cassava pottage with salt-cured beef

Chibé, one of the most traditional dishes of the Amazon region, is the staple food of many people and is made from cassava flour and water. This simple base can be eaten by itself, as an appetizer or as a main dish with several accompaniments. It can also be served for dessert, sweetened with rapadura sugar. Jacuba is another name for chibé, and different regions of Brazil consume it in different consistencies, from liquid to thick. Fishermen always carry a bag of cassava flour with them to prepare an improvised chibé while at sea or by the river, to accompany the fish they grill on their own boat. They named this combination avuado.

Serves 4

* 500g forequarter charque or other Brazilian-style salt-cured beef, cut into 2cm cubes
* 100g farinha-d'água or fine, untoasted cassava flour
* 1 litre ice-cold bottled still water
* salt
* 80g red onion, finely chopped
* 2 tbsp finely chopped culantro (Mexican/long coriander)
* 2 tbsp finely chopped coriander leaves
* 2 tbsp chopped pimenta-de-cheiro or other mild chilli
* 2 cumari-do-pará or other mild yellow chillies, deseeded and chopped
* 60ml lime juice

1. Put the charque cubes in a large bowl and cover with cold water. Soak for 12 hours in the refrigerator, changing the water every 3 hours to remove excess salt.

2. Drain the meat and put in a saucepan with 1.5 litres of fresh water. Cook for 1 hour over a medium-low heat or until the charque is tender. Drain the meat.

3. Preheat a grill or barbecue, then cook the charque for 1 minute on each side, placing it 30cm from the heat source. Set aside.

4. Put the farinha-d'água in a bowl and cover with the cold bottled water. Leave to stand for 5 minutes. Season to taste with salt, then add the remaining ingredients, stirring well to combine.

5. Divide the chibé among four bowls and arrange three pieces of meat on top of each to serve.

Tips from Thiago:
Chibé is also the perfect accompaniment to Chargrilled Fish Ribs (see page 114).

Terrina de rabada com pupunha
Oxtail terrine with peach palm fruit

Oxtail is one of the best beef cuts but is considered by many Brazilians to be second rate because it contains bones. Rabada, an oxtail stew, has suffered a lot of prejudice in the past but is now making a return to our tables in great style. If you can't find fresh peach palm fruit, you can substitute with pumpkin, or use cans of brined peach palm fruit, which are sold as pejivalles or chontaduros in Latin American stores – omit the salt if that is the case.

Serves 4

* 1 tbsp crushed garlic, plus 1 tbsp chopped garlic
* 140g onion, chopped
* ½ tsp ground black pepper
* ½ tsp ground cumin
* 200ml stout
* salt
* 2.5kg oxtail pieces
* 30ml extra virgin olive oil
* 80g tomato, chopped
* 1 tbsp ground annatto (achiote) seeds

* 60g carrot, cut into large cubes
* 1 tbsp chopped pimenta-de-cheiro or other mild chilli
* 4 bay leaves
* 2 tbsp hand-torn culantro (Mexican/long coriander)
* 2 tbsp hand-torn basil

Peach palm fruit
* 600g whole, fresh peach palm fruit
* butter
* 1 tbsp rosemary leaves

1. Make a marinade by combining the crushed garlic, 60g of the chopped onion, the black pepper, cumin, stout and 20g of salt in a blender and process to a paste. Put the oxtail in a non-reactive dish, add the marinade and toss well. Refrigerate for 4 hours.

2. Heat the olive oil in a heavy-based saucepan and sauté the remaining 80g onion and the chopped garlic with the tomato, ground annatto, carrots and chilli until the vegetables are softened.

3. Add the oxtail and bay leaves and cook over a low heat for 5 minutes, then cover and cook for a further 5 minutes to release the meat juices.

4. Reduce the heat to very low and braise for 4–5 hours, stirring every 15 minutes and checking the level of liquid in the pan. Add water little by little during the cooking time if the meat juices begin to dry out. After 2 hours of braising, stir in the culantro and basil, cover again and continue cooking.

5. To cook the peach palm fruit, put them in a large saucepan with 20g of salt and cover with cold water. Bring to the boil and cook for 40–50 minutes until they are fork tender. Drain, then peel the fruit, cut them in half and discard the pit. Reserve 100g of the fruit to dry in the oven.

6. Melt 1 tablespoon of butter in a frying pan. Add the rosemary and remaining peach palm fruit and cook, stirring, for 1 minute. Set aside.

7. Preheat the oven to 120°C (250°F), gas mark ¼. Finely grate the reserved peach palm fruit and spread it on a baking sheet. Place in the oven to dry for 20 minutes.

8. Melt 10g of butter in a frying pan and add the oven-dried peach palm fruit. Cook, stirring constantly, until crunchy. Set aside.

9. When the oxtail is cooked, transfer it to a tray to cool slightly. Set aside the pan of sauce.

10. Pull the meat off the bones, retaining the bones. Pack the meat into a loaf tin measuring about 18 x 7cm. Place another loaf tin the same size on top and press down gently. Sit a can of food or another heavy object inside the top tin to weigh it down.

11. Refrigerate the oxtail terrine for 3 hours to allow the gelatine to set and bind the pieces of meat together.

12. Meanwhile, return the oxtail bones to the pan of sauce. Add 1 litre of water, bring to the boil and simmer for 30 minutes. Strain, then set aside the sauce to thicken naturally.

13. Preheat the oven to 120°C (250°F), gas mark ¼. Remove the terrine from the refrigerator and turn it out. Cut into cubes about 6cm wide. Transfer to a baking sheet and bake for 10 minutes.

14. Serve the terrine, drizzled with the reduced sauce and accompanied with the sautéed peach palm fruit and the toasted flour.

Carnes e aves para o fogo e a grelha } *Meat and poultry for fire and grill*

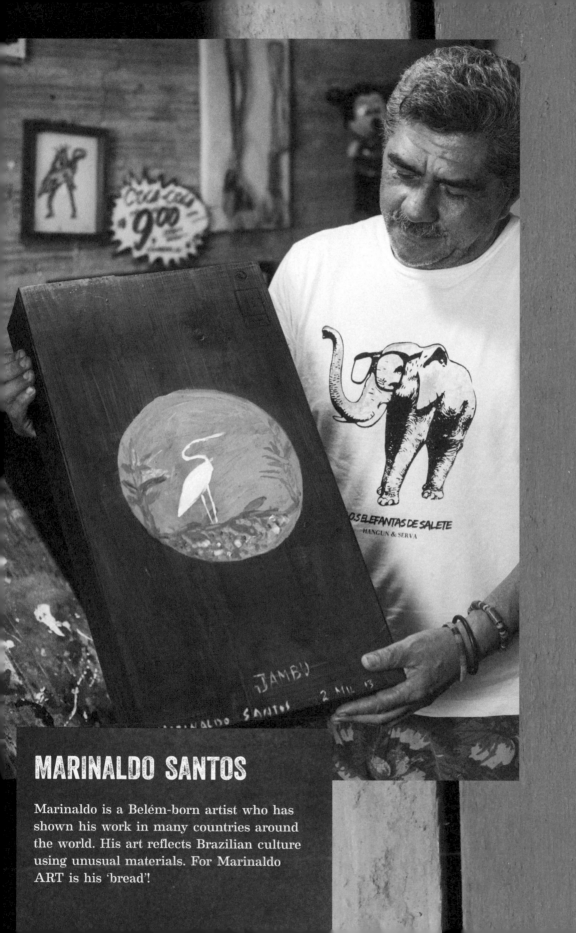

MARINALDO SANTOS

Marinaldo is a Belém-born artist who has
shown his work in many countries around
the world. His art reflects Brazilian culture
using unusual materials. For Marinaldo
ART is his 'bread'!

DIOGO PINHO

Diogo is one of the most talented chefs at the restaurant Remanso do Bosque. His love for bread began as a hobby and turned into a passion. For Diogo BREAD is his art!

Pão de milho
Corn bread

Serves 4

* 750g plain flour, plus extra for dusting
* 100g coarse polenta or cornmeal
* 1 tbsp salt
* 20g caster sugar
* ½ tbsp active dried yeast
* 1 small egg
* 20g butter, plus extra for greasing
* 50g starter or pâte fermentée (see tips, below)
* ½ tbsp fennel seeds

1. Put the plain flour, polenta, salt, sugar and yeast in the bowl of an electric mixer. Turn it to a low speed and mix until the ingredients are well combined.

2 Add the egg, butter, starter and 300ml of water. Knead on a medium speed for 8–10 minutes.

3. Remove the dough from the bowl, place in a large bowl, cover with a tea towel and leave to rise in a warm place for 40 minutes until doubled in size.

4. Preheat the oven to 170°C (340°F), gas mark 3½. Grease and flour a 20 x 10cm loaf tin.

5. Add the fennel seeds to the proven dough and knead to incorporate. Shape the dough into a log and place it in the tin.

6. Bake for 20 minutes or until golden all over the top, then remove the bread from the tin and serve with Smoked Butter with Cocoa Nibs (see page 98).

Tips from Diogo:
This recipe will only work if you use a starter, pâte fermentée or 'mother' dough. If you do not have a starter, ask a local baker if they can offer you a piece, so you can start your own.

Pão de mandioca
Cassava bread

Diogo, the sous-chef at Remanso do Bosque restaurant (see page 201), embraced a passion for breadmaking and became a great baker. His invention and experimentation have resulted in many recipes. One day, he decided to adapt a classic recipe for potato bread using cassava instead, and to his surprise the bread rose to almost twice the expected size! From then on, he started to use cassava to improve many of the traditional bread recipes. Here is that 'miraculous' recipe.

Makes 1 large loaf

* 700g raw cassava roots, peeled and roughly chopped
* 1.5kg plain flour, plus extra for dusting
* 80g caster sugar
* 20g salt
* 15g active dried yeast
* oil, for greasing

Tips from Diogo:
If you can't find raw cassava roots you can use frozen ones instead, in which case cook them gently in water for 1 hour over a low heat.

1. Put the cassava in a saucepan with 2 litres of water and simmer for 10–15 minutes or until fork tender. Remove the cassava from the pan and mash them through a potato ricer. Set aside 700ml of the cooking liquid to cool.

2. In a large bowl, combine the flour, mashed cassava, sugar, salt, yeast and the reserved 700ml cooking liquid. Bring together with your hands to form a smooth dough.

3. Turn the dough onto a clean, floured surface and knead for 10 minutes until it is smooth and elastic.

4. Return the dough to the bowl, cover with a clean, damp tea towel and leave to rise for 1½ hours.

5. Oil and flour a large deep baking tin or roasting tin measuring about 55 x 30 x 10cm. Remove the dough from the bowl, punch down to expel the gases and pat it out into the prepared tin. Dust the top with a little more flour and leave to rise again for a further 30 minutes.

6. Preheat the oven to 200°C (400°F), gas mark 6. Put half a cup of water in a small baking tin and put it on the floor of the oven; the steam formed will give the bread a nice crisp crust. Bake the bread for 30 minutes.

7. Remove the bread from the tin and leave to cool on a wire rack to prevent it sweating. Serve hot with Smoked Butter with Cocoa Nibs (see page 98).

Pães de tapioca e queijo coalho na folha

Leaf-wrapped cassava and cheese rolls

Puxuri is an Amazonian seed, also known as noz do Pará (Pará nut). It has valuable medicinal properties and is often used in perfumery. Despite being little known for its culinary uses, it is a delightful spice and can be used as a substitute for nutmeg.

Makes 15

* 500ml unsweetened coconut milk
* 250g Farinha de Tapioca (or see page 82)
* 200g queijo de coalho or halloumi cheese, grated
* 1 tsp grated puxuri or nutmeg
* 5g salt
* 1 large free-range egg
* 6 guarimã leaves (see tips, below)

1. Bring the coconut milk to scalding point in a small saucepan. Meanwhile, combine the farinha de tapioca, cheese, puxuri and salt in a mixing bowl.

2. Pour the hot coconut milk over the tapioca and cheese mixture and stir well. Leave to cool slightly then add the egg, mixing until combined. Leave to stand for 20 minutes.

3. Cut the guarimã leaves into 12cm squares and set aside.

4. Roll the dough into 8cm balls and pat them into ovals. Wrap each one in a square of guarimã leaf, pressing gently to make it stick to the surface.

5. Preheat the oven to 200°C (400°F), gas mark 6 and preheat a cast-iron frying pan or griddle pan on the stove. Part-cook the dough parcels in the hot pan to impart a toasted flavour, then transfer them to a baking sheet and bake in the oven for 30 minutes. Serve hot with black coffee.

Tips from Thiago:
If you cannot find guarimã leaves, use banana leaves instead. Or, if you prefer to cook them without wrapping, just place the rolls on a baking sheet and bake for 30 minutes at the same temperature.

Pão de queijo
Cheese rolls

This recipe from Fred (see page 166) is a speciality from the Minas Gerais state and has become part of Brazilian everyday life. It is sold in bars, and served at breakfast in hotels, airport coffee shops, as well as in homes. Although the word pão ('bread' in Portuguese) features in the name, there is no yeast or baking powder in the dough. Its elasticity and the leavening action come from the mixture of sour cassava flour and cheese. These rolls are irresistible straight from the oven.

Makes 15

* 280g queijo da Canastra meia-cura or other mild firm cheese such as gruyère
* 320g polvilho azedo (sour cassava starch)
* 150ml whipping cream, at room temperature
* 150ml whole milk, at room temperature
* 150g butter, at room temperature
* salt

1. Preheat the oven to 200°C (400°F), gas mark 6. Finely grate the cheese and set aside.

2. Sift the sour cassava flour into a bowl and add the cream, milk, butter and grated cheese. Add a little salt, bearing in mind how salty the cheese is that you are using. Knead by hand until the dough is smooth and elastic.

3. Line a baking sheet with parchment paper. Roll the dough into 8cm balls and put them on the prepared baking tray, leaving enough room between them to expand as they bake.

4. Bake for 30–40 minutes or until they are a light golden brown. Serve hot.

Tips from Felipe:
The cooking time will change depending on the size of the rolls. They should be baked until they begin to colour, but are still elastic in the centre. In Minas Gerais, they are usually served in a basket made of corn husks, accompanied by a freshly brewed coffee sweetened with rapadura sugar. This dough freezes well.

Sweet cassava griddle cakes

BEIJU

Beiju is a gluten-free speciality of tupi-guarani indigenous origins that can be prepared in various forms such as crêpes (see page 55) or as a flatbread or griddle cakes, as pictured here. The main ingredient is always tapioca flour or cassava flour. However, there are hundreds of different types and names of beijus throughout Brazil.

Sour dough
griddle cakes

Cassava flatbread

Beiju de massa doce

Sweet cassava griddle cakes

Makes 10

* 400g unwaxed, unpeeled, raw cassava roots
* 2 banana leaves
* 50g finely shredded desiccated coconut
* 1 tonka bean, grated
* ½ tsp fennel seeds
* 40g caster sugar
* salt

1. Put the unpeeled cassava roots in a bowl, add cold water to cover and leave to soak for 3 days.

2. When ready to cook, cut the banana leaf into 10 pieces measuring 25 x 22cm and set aside.

3. Peel the soaked cassava root and finely grate it. Combine with the coconut, tonka bean, fennel seeds, sugar and salt to taste.

4. Place a 50g portion of the mixture in the centre of each piece of banana leaf and fold into a parcel. Use a little of the mixture to seal.

5. Preheat a cast-iron frying pan or a griddle pan and cook the parcels until the leaves turn brown. Serve immediately.

Tips from Thiago:
If you cannot find unwaxed cassava roots, peel them before soaking in water.

Beiju de farinha azeda

Sour dough griddle cakes

Makes 10

* 2 banana leaves
* 170g farinha-d'água or untoasted cassava flour
* 50g unsweetened, finely shredded desiccated coconut
* ½ tsp salt

1. Cut the banana leaf into 10 pieces measuring 25 x 22cm and set aside.

2. Combine the farinha-d'água, coconut and salt in a bowl and set aside.

3. Bring 350ml of water to the boil in a saucepan and pour over the farinha mixture. Stir to combine, then leave to stand for 20 minutes.

4. Place a 30g portion of the dough in the centre of each piece of banana leaf. Fold into a parcel, pressing down slightly so that each package is about 1.5cm high.

5. Preheat a cast-iron frying pan or griddle pan and cook the parcels until the leaves are blackened. Serve immediately.

Beiju cica

Cassava flatbread

Makes 10

* 80g farinha de suruí or fine, untoasted cassava flour
* 80g farinha de carimã or fine, untoasted cassava flour
* salt

1. Combine the farinha de suruí, farinha de carimã and a little salt in a mixing bowl.

2. Bring 180ml of water to the boil in a saucepan and pour over the farinha mixture. As soon as it is cool enough to handle, knead by hand to form a smooth dough. Leave to stand for 15 minutes.

3. Divide the dough into 15g portions. Cut a 30cm square of cling film and place one portion of dough in the centre. Cover with another 30cm square of cling film.

4. Use a rolling pin to roll the dough into a 1cm-thick disc. Peel the cling film from the disc and repeat with the remaining dough.

5. Preheat a cast-iron frying pan and cook the discs of dough, one at a time, for 1 minute on each side or until they are golden brown. Be careful not to let them scorch. Serve immediately.

NENA

Nena is an Amazonian food heroine, who follows a family tradition of organic chocolate making at home. Her chocolate is called Filhos do Combu (Sons of Combu), as it is produced on Combu Island in the Amazon rainforest, only 1.5 kilometres from Belém.

SWEET TREATS

MAKING CHOCOLATE IN THE JUNGLE

While Belém is a city with classic urban characteristics, Combu Island, only 10 minutes away by boat, maintains the peculiarities of a riverside life.

On one of my visits to Combu I met Nena, who became my main producer of chocolate and a good friend. For her, the process of making chocolate is more than a job, it is a way of living.

Nena's home and chocolate factory is in a house with an entrance on stilts. You can only reach her by boat. Her backyard is the Amazonian rainforest, and instead of herbs and vegetables, she has cocoa and açai trees in her 'garden'.

There is a sense of purity and innocence in her work. There is no distraction, except nature itself, and Nena puts her heart and soul into each chocolate bar she produces.

She harvests the cocoa pods one by one, then takes the seeds (each pod has between 20-50 seeds) and performs each step manually to create the final product, which she wraps in cocoa leaves. The result is a pure chocolate with cocoa nibs.

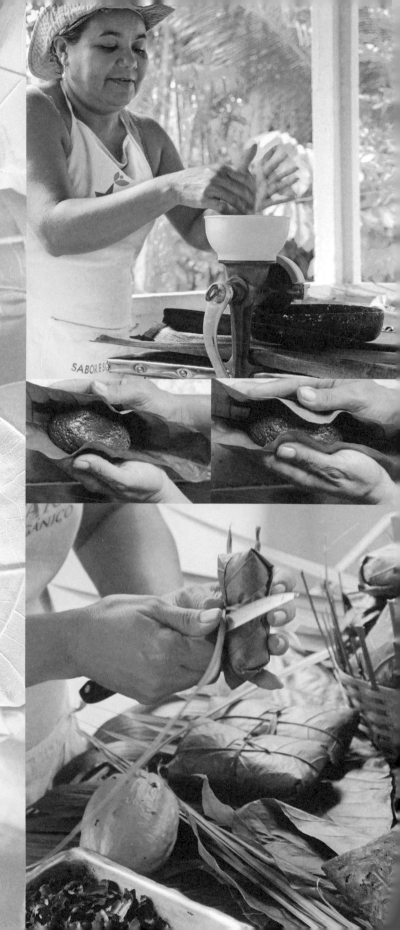

Bolo de chocolate com cupuaçu
Chocolate cake with cupuaçu

Chocolate and cupuaçu is a classic combination of the Amazon region. Cupuaçu truffles have broken through class barriers and are now sold on the streets as well as in the finest bakeries in the country. This chilled cake is an attempt to reproduce the idea behind these truffles. You can find frozen cupuaçu pulp in Brazilian, Asian and African food shops.

Serves 10

* 5 large eggs
* 290g caster sugar
* 340g plain chocolate, about 50% cocoa solids, chopped
* 225g unsalted butter, diced at room temperature
* 150g plain flour, sifted
* oil, for greasing

Cupuaçu preserve

* 150g cupuaçu pulp or ripe pineapple or mango flesh
* 150g caster sugar

Chocolate mousse

* 4 egg yolks, plus 5 egg whites
* 100g caster sugar
* 250g plain chocolate, about 50% cocoa solids, chopped
* 200g butter
* 50g cocoa nibs, chopped

1. Using an electric hand mixer, beat the 5 eggs with 100g of the sugar for 8 minutes or until light and fluffy, then refrigerate.

2. Prepare a syrup. Combine 100ml of water and 190g of sugar in a saucepan and heat for 4 minutes until the sugar has dissolved. Remove from the heat and add the chopped chocolate and diced butter. Leave to stand for 1 minute.

3. Using a wire whisk, gradually beat the flour into the syrup, mixing until all the chocolate and butter are well incorporated. Refrigerate for 30 minutes.

4. Preheat the oven to 110°C (225°F), gas mark ¼. Oil a 20 x 10cm loaf tin and line it with parchment paper.

5. Using a silicone spatula, gently fold the chocolate mixture into the whipped eggs. Pour the batter into the prepared tin and bake for 50 minutes.

6. Let the cake cool in the tin, then refrigerate for 4 hours. Carefully turn the cake onto a plate. Peel off the parchment paper and cut the cake into large cubes. Set aside.

7. To make the cupuaçu preserve, combine the cupuaçu pulp and sugar in a heavy saucepan and cook over a low heat for 15 minutes, stirring constantly with a wooden spoon, until the mixture turns golden brown. Remove from the heat, transfer to a sterilized glass jar and leave to cool. Do not refrigerate, as the preserve will crystallize.

8. To make the chocolate mousse, combine the egg yolks and sugar in a double boiler and cook, beating constantly with a wire whisk, until the mixture is light and fluffy. Remove from the heat and set aside.

9. Melt the chocolate and butter together in a double boiler, or in a microwave oven for 30 seconds. Whisk this mixture into the egg mixture, then refrigerate for 20 minutes.

10. Using an electric hand mixer, whisk the egg whites until stiff peaks form. Fold the whisked egg whites into the chocolate mixture, stirring carefully with a silicone spatula to avoid deflating the whites.

11. Carefully fold the cocoa nibs into the mousse. Refrigerate for 2 hours before serving.

12. Place a scoop of chocolate mousse on a serving plate. Sit a cube of chocolate cake beside it. Add 1 tablespoon of cupuaçu preserve and serve.

Pudim de fruta-pão
Breadfruit pudding

Bread pudding is an unpretentious dessert that is enjoyed in many countries, each of which has its own version. As we in the Amazon have a fruit called breadfruit, I thought I'd play with the idea of the name and create something different, more like a caramel custard, served in individual moulds.

Serves 6

* 250g breadfruit seeds
* 300ml whole milk
* 4 eggs
* 395g sweetened condensed milk
* 200g caster sugar
* 1 tsp vanilla extract

To decorate (optional)
* breadfruit seeds, peeled
* spun sugar

1. Cook the breadfruit seeds for 20 minutes in a saucepan of boiling water.

2. Drain the breadfruit seeds and plunge them into cold water. Leave to soak for 30 minutes, to make it easier to remove the skins, then peel them.

3. Preheat the oven to 180°C (350°F), gas mark 4. Process the seeds in a blender with the milk, eggs, condensed milk, 40g of the sugar and the vanilla extract for about 2 minutes or until smooth. Set aside.

4. Heat the remaining sugar in a saucepan over a low heat until it melts and turns into a golden caramel. Remove from the heat and swirl 2 tablespoons of the caramel in each of six dariole moulds or similar individual moulds.

5. Carefully pour the breadfruit mixture into the moulds and cover with foil. Transfer them to a roasting tin. Pour hot water into the tin so that it comes halfway up the sides of the moulds. Bake for 40 minutes or until just set.

6. Remove the puddings from the oven and leave to cool, then refrigerate for at least 2 hours before turning out and serving with breadfruit and spun sugar (if using).

FELIPE CASTANHO

My younger brother, Felipe, decided to study gastronomy at SENAC Campos do Jordão, following in my footsteps. He graduated recently, but is already very experienced in the kitchen, working at our restaurant Remanso do Bosque in Belém, Pará. He has a special interest in the pastry area, and some of our desserts are his creations. Felipe is also a very talented organizer, and is getting ready to head our business. He is my right hand and plays a very important part in the success of our restaurants.

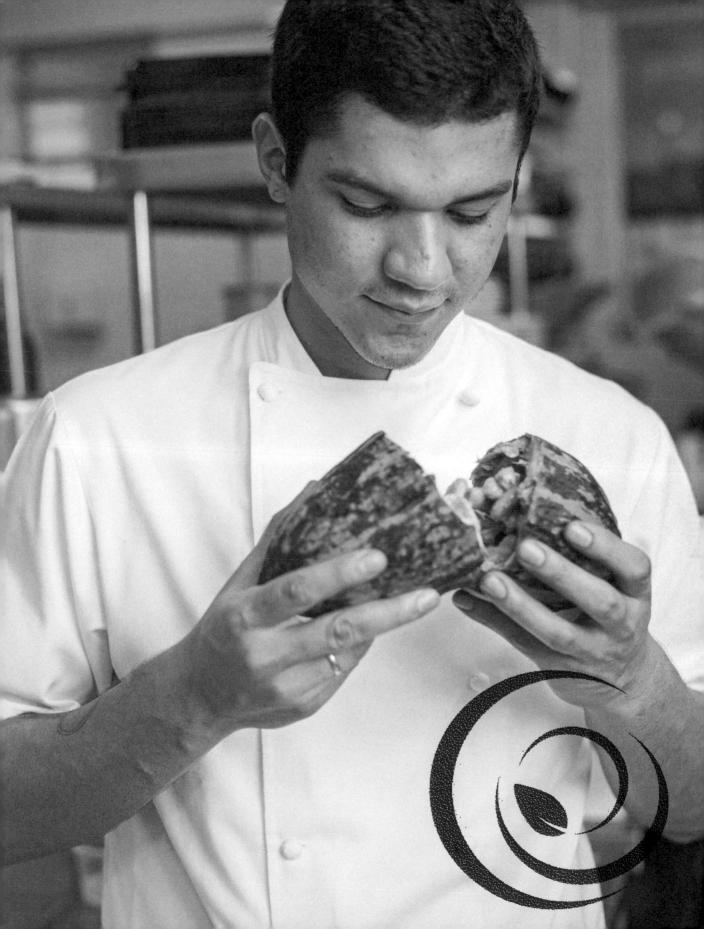

Crumble de banana
Banana crumble

We Brazilians see crumble, which was introduced to our country by the Europeans, as a sweet version of farofa. In our cuisine crumble can be served as a stand-alone product, used as a topping for cakes and desserts or combined with fruit – banana is the most popular flavour. This crumble mixture can be sprinkled on top of a sponge cake before baking to give it a crunchy top, but I prepare it without the cake.

Serves 8

* 50g cold unsalted butter, plus extra for greasing
* 100g plain flour, plus extra for dusting
* 100g caster sugar
* 25g Brazil nut meal
* 12 ripe bananas (about 1.5kg)
* ground cinnamon

1. Preheat the oven to 200°C (400°F), gas mark 6. Grease and flour a 30 x 20cm baking dish.

2. Combine the flour, sugar, butter and Brazil nut meal in a bowl and work the mixture with your fingertips until it resembles fine breadcrumbs – be careful not to overmix. Set aside.

3. Peel the bananas and cut them in half lengthways. Arrange them in the prepared tin, pressing them down slightly. Sprinkle with ground cinnamon to taste and cover with the crumble mixture.

4. Bake for 10 minutes, then lower the oven temperature to 150°C (300°F), gas mark 2, and continue baking for a further 10 minutes. The surface should be golden brown all over when ready. Serve hot.

Tips from Thiago:
If you cannot find Brazil nut meal, it is easy to prepare at home – simply grind the nuts to a fine powder in a food processor. This recipe is great served with Tapioca and Vanilla Ice Cream (see page 238).

'Bolo podre' com calda de café e tapioca caramelizada

Tapioca pudding with coffee syrup and caramelized tapioca

This is a traditional pudding of the Amazon region. It does not contain wheat but granulated tapioca flakes, usually moistened with coconut milk. We eat it in the morning, or late afternoon, always accompanied by a cup of freshly brewed coffee.

Serves 10

* 2 vanilla pods
* 50g unsweetened, finely shredded desiccated coconut
* 500ml whole milk
* 200g sweetened condensed milk
* 100ml unsweetened coconut milk
* 120g farinha de tapioca (granulated tapioca) or Farinha de Tapioca substitute (see page 82)
* oil, for greasing

Coffee syrup

* 80g rapadura or dark muscovado sugar
* 250ml hot espresso coffee

Caramelized tapioca

* 100g farinha de tapioca (granulated tapioca) or Farinha de Tapioca substitute (see page 82)
* 60g caster sugar

1. Cut the vanilla pods in half lengthways and scrape out the seeds with the tip of a knife. Put the seeds, pods, desiccated coconut and all the milks in a saucepan. Place over a medium heat and cook, stirring constantly, until the mixture reaches scalding point. Discard the vanilla pods.

2. Put the farinha de tapioca in a large bowl and pour the hot milk mixture over it. Mix well. Pour the batter into a generously oiled 30 x 11cm loaf tin and refrigerate for 3 hours or until firm.

3. To make the coffee syrup, combine the rapadura and 60ml of water in a saucepan. Heat for 2 minutes, stirring until the rapadura has dissolved. Add the coffee and remove from the heat.

4. For the caramelized tapioca, combine the farinha de tapioca and sugar in a saucepan and heat gently, stirring constantly, to melt the sugar. Cook until the caramel is a light golden brown. Pour the mixture onto a nonstick baking sheet and leave to cool. Store in an airtight container.

5. Turn the chilled cake out onto a serving board and sprinkle with the caramelized tapioca. Serve in slices, accompanied by a drizzle of coffee syrup.

Tips from Thiago:
When pouring the pudding batter into the tin, press it down gently to pack it together and prevent it from falling apart when it is removed from the tin.

Tiramisù de bacuri
Platonia tiramisu

The bacuri, or platonia as it is known in English, has a juicy, sweet and sour pulp that is rich in phosphorus, calcium and potassium. Both the pulp and the husk are used in cooking, and the oil extracted from the seeds is used by the pharmaceutical and cosmetics industries. The tree can reach over 30 metres in height, and it takes at least 10 years to bear its first fruits. You can find frozen and sometimes fresh bacuri in Brazilian and Asian food shops and markets.

Serves 8

Coffee syrup
* 400ml unsweetened espresso coffee
* 100g caster sugar
* 2 tbsp cachaça
* 4 tbsp lime juice
* 1 tbsp rosemary leaves
* 3 tbsp sweetened condensed milk

Tiramisu
* 3 eggs, separated
* 210g caster sugar
* 3 tbsp cachaça
* 300g chilled whipping cream
* 300g creamy queijo do Marajó or mascarpone
* 200g bacuri (platonia) pulp or lychees, deseeded
* 30 ladyfinger biscuits
* 8 tbsp cocoa powder

1. To make the syrup, combine the coffee, sugar, cachaça, lime juice, rosemary and 100ml of water in a saucepan. Heat over a low heat for 4 minutes until the sugar has dissolved – do not allow it to boil.

2. Leave the syrup to cool, then add the condensed milk, stirring well to combine. Set aside.

3. To make the tiramisu, in a large heatproof bowl whisk the egg yolks with 150g of the sugar until light, pale and creamy.

4. Add the cachaça and place the yolk mixture in a double boiler or over a pan of steaming water. Whisk constantly for 3 minutes or until the mixture doubles in volume. Remove from the heat and leave to cool, then refrigerate for 3 hours.

5. In an electric mixer, whip the cream with 20g of the sugar for about 4 minutes, being careful not to over whip. Keep refrigerated.

6. Cut the queijo do Marajó into pieces and place in a blender with the bacuri pulp. Blend until it forms a smooth cream. Set aside.

7. In a large clean bowl, whisk the egg whites with the remaining 40g of the sugar until it forms stiff peaks.

8. Using a rubber spatula, fold the egg yolk mixture, bacuri cream and whipped cream into the egg whites, being careful not to deflate the mixture.

9. Spoon a layer of the tiramisu mixture into a glass serving dish, then add a layer of ladyfingers, dipping them very briefly in the coffee syrup before putting them in the dish.

10. Reserve some of the cocoa powder to decorate the tiramisu, then sprinkle some of the rest over the ladyfingers. Repeat the layers until the ingredients are all used up. Finish with a layer of cream and the reserved cocoa. Refrigerate the dessert for at least 2 hours before serving.

Bolinho de tapioca com toffee de cumaru

Cassava cakes with tonka bean caramel

I have great affection for this recipe because it reminds me a lot of my childhood, when I used to go to my grandmother's house for the weekend. She prepared these little cakes in the morning and an unforgettable aroma always came out of the oven. The recipe is easy. We added to this version a caramel sauce made with cumaru, known in English as tonka bean – an aromatic Amazonian seed used in folk medicine and perfumery, and now also used for cooking.

Makes 10

Tonka bean caramel
* 500ml single cream
* 500g caster sugar
* 2 tonka bean pods or vanilla pods
* 100g unsalted butter
* ¼ tsp sea salt flakes

Cassava cakes
* oil, for greasing
* 470g farinha de tapioca or Farinha de Tapioca Substitute (see page 82)
* 45g butter, at room temperature
* 70g caster sugar
* 30g queijo de coalho or halloumi, grated
* 2 pinches of salt
* 500ml whole milk
* 1 free-range egg
* 1 tsp fennel seeds

Tips from Thiago:
If substituting halloumi for queijo de coalho, omit the salt in the cake batter. This recipe can also be served with Tapioca and Vanilla Ice Cream (see page 238) or plain vanilla ice cream.

1. To make the caramel, melt the sugar slowly in a heavy-based stainless steel saucepan. In a separate saucepan, heat the cream to scalding point.

2. When the sugar has turned to a golden caramel, or reached 170°C on a sugar thermometer, pour the hot cream into it and add the tonka bean pods.

3. Continue cooking until the caramel sauce coats the back of a spoon, then remove the pan from the heat.

4. Stir the butter and sea salt flakes into the sauce, then transfer to a blender and process for 2 minutes. Pass the caramel through a sieve. Leave to cool, then store in a sealed container in the refrigerator.

5. Next make the cassava cakes. Preheat the oven to 180°C (350°F), gas mark 4, and oil a large baking sheet.

6. In a large bowl, combine the tapioca flour with the butter, sugar, cheese and salt.

7. In a saucepan, heat the milk to 80°C and pour it over the flour mixture. Stir well, then leave to stand for about 30 minutes.

8. When the mixture has cooled, add the egg and fennel seeds and mix well.

9. Shape the dough into balls the size of golf balls, then put them on the prepared baking sheet and bake for 20 minutes. Serve the cakes while still warm with some of the reheated caramel.

Sopa fria de maracujá com pimenta e farinha de pipoca

Cold passion fruit soup with chilli and popcorn flour

I have learned from the Portuguese chef Vitor Sobral how to thicken sauces, soups and purées using vegetables, eliminating the need to add fat. In this delicious dessert recipe, we use carrots to thicken the passion fruit soup, which makes it very healthy.

Serves 6

* 300g carrots, peeled and thickly sliced
* 160g caster sugar
* 200g fresh passion fruit pulp
* 1 cumari-do-Pará or other mild yellow chilli, deseeded

Passion fruit jam

* 1kg whole passion fruit
* 200g caster sugar

Popcorn flour

* 1 tbsp vegetable oil
* 100g popcorn kernels

1. Put the carrots in a saucepan with the sugar and 900ml of water. Bring to the boil and cook for 20 minutes or until the carrots are very tender. Strain, reserving the cooking liquid.

2. Combine the cooked carrots, passion fruit pulp, chilli and 200ml of the carrot cooking liquid in a blender. Blitz for 5 minutes to give a very smooth cream. Refrigerate for 2 hours.

3. To make the jam, cut the passion fruit open and scrape out the pulp and seeds. Set aside.

4. Scrape the white pith from inside the shells and put it in a blender. Add 400ml of water and process until combined. Strain the liquid into a saucepan.

5. Add the passion fruit pulp and sugar to the saucepan and place over a low heat. Cook for 12 minutes, stirring constantly with a wooden spoon, until a jammy consistency forms.

6. Pour the jam into a sterilized glass jar. Leave to cool completely, then seal and keep refrigerated.

7. To make the popcorn flour, heat the oil in a large saucepan, add the corn kernels, cover and cook, shaking the pan, until they have popped. Leave to cool completely. Put the cooled, popped corn in a blender or food processor and process to a fine flour.

8. To serve, put a ladleful of passion fruit soup into a soup plate. Decorate with 2 tablespoons of passion fruit jam and sprinkle with a little popcorn flour.

Bolo de fubá

Polenta cake

Some recipes are synonymous with comfort and bring us happy memories of childhood. My grandmother (on my mother's side) served this cake for breakfast.

Serves 6

* 75g unsalted butter, at room temperature, plus extra for greasing
* 120g fubá or super-fine yellow polenta, plus extra for dusting
* 4 eggs, separated
* 360g caster sugar
* 240g plain flour
* 4 tsp baking powder
* 250ml whole milk

1. Preheat the oven to 180°C (350°F), gas mark 4. Grease a loaf tin and dust with sifted polenta meal.

2. In a large bowl, whisk the egg whites until frothy using an electric hand mixer. Gradually add the sugar and continue whisking until firm peaks form. Set aside.

3. Sift together the flour, baking powder and fubá or polenta. Set aside.

4. Beat together the butter and egg yolks until light and fluffy. Stir in the milk, then add the dry ingredients and beat until smooth.

5. Fold the whisked egg whites into the batter using slow movements until well incorporated.

6. Pour the batter into the prepared tin and bake for about 30 minutes or until a skewer inserted in the centre of the cake comes out clean.

Tips from Thiago:
The original cake is made with fubá, a very fine cornmeal available at Brazilian shops. If you are using polenta or other cornmeal instead, remember the finer the texture, the better.

{

Mingau de tapioca com sorbet de banana-da-terra

Pará-style tapioca pudding with plantain sorbet

At Ver-o-Peso market, there are several stalls selling delicious tapioca puddings. In the mornings, when I go there to shop for ingredients, I begin my day by eating one of them, served with pieces of sweet, ripe plantain. In this recipe, the plantain takes the form of a sorbet.

Serves 4

* 80g tapioca
* 400ml whole milk
* 100ml cream
* 100g caster sugar
* pinch of salt
* 1 cinnamon stick
* 4 scoops Plantain and Lime Sorbet (see page 242)

Cinnamon oil

* 60ml coconut oil
* 1 cinnamon stick
* 3g ground cinnamon

Banana leather

* 400g ripe bananas, unpeeled
* sea salt flakes

Tips from Thiago:
If you do not have a silicone mat, I highly recommend you buy one. It is a long-lasting tool that replaces parchment paper in baking and other dishes cooked in the oven.

1. Combine the tapioca, milk, cream, sugar, salt and cinnamon stick in a saucepan and bring to the boil. Cook for 5 minutes, stirring constantly. Remove the pan from the heat and leave it to cool, then refrigerate for 3 hours.

2. To make the cinnamon oil, combine the coconut oil, cinnamon stick and ground cinnamon in a small pan and heat over a low heat for 5 minutes – do not let the temperature reach 60°C. Remove from the heat and transfer to a sterilized bottle to store.

3. To make the banana leather, preheat the oven to 180°C (350°F), gas mark 4. Put the unpeeled bananas on a baking sheet and bake for 15 minutes. Remove the bananas from the oven and reduce the temperature to 110°C (225°F), gas mark ¼.

4. Peel the bananas and put the flesh in a blender with 100ml of water. Blitz until the mixture is very smooth.

5. Put a silicone mat on a baking sheet and spread the banana purée over it using an icing spatula to form a uniform, paper-thin layer. Sprinkle with sea salt flakes, then bake for 40 minutes.

6. Remove the banana leather from the oven and carefully peel it from the silicone mat. Break into smaller pieces and store in an airtight container until needed.

7. To serve, place 2 spoonfuls of tapioca pudding in a bowl. Top with a scoop of plantain sorbet and drizzle with the cinnamon oil. Decorate with the banana leather and serve immediately.

Sorvete de tapioca com baunilha
Tapioca and vanilla ice cream

Serves 6

* **1 vanilla pod, preferably Amazonian**
* **500ml whole milk**
* **200g double cream**
* **100g farinha de tapioca or granulated tapioca or Farinha de Tapioca Substitute (see page 82)**
* **200g granulated sugar**

1. Using a sharp knife, split the vanilla pod in half lengthways and scrape out the seeds.

2. Bring the milk to scalding point in a medium saucepan, then remove from the heat. Add the vanilla seeds and pods, plus the cream and granulated tapioca. Leave to stand for 15 minutes.

3. In a separate saucepan, combine the sugar with 100ml of water. Heat, stirring, until the sugar has dissolved, then cook for 7 minutes until forms a thin syrup. Leave to cool completely.

4. Pour the cooled syrup into the tapioca mixture and refrigerate for 2 hours.

5. Churn in an ice cream machine following the manufacturer's instructions, then freeze for 2 hours before serving.

Tips from Thiago:
If you don't have an ice cream machine, transfer the mixture to a freezer-proof bowl and put it in the freezer. Every 30 minutes, remove the bowl from the freezer and whisk the contents with a wire whisk. Repeat the procedure five times until the mixture has frozen, then leave the ice cream in the freezer for 2 hours before serving. This process simulates that of an ice cream machine, helping to break the larger ice crystals that form during slower freezing.

Sorbet de açaí com melaço de cana
Açai sorbet with black treacle

The açai berry is a small purple fruit that grows on a high palm tree native to the Amazon floodplain. In Brazil, açai palm trees are grown in several states, with Pará leading the national production. Growing açai is one of the main income-generating activities for the riverside population. The increasing appreciation of this fruit worldwide has had a positive ecological impact on the region, as these trees are no longer being cut down to extract hearts of palm. Packed with antioxidants, fibre and minerals, the açai berry is known around the world as a superfood of high nutritional value. The taste suggests a mix of red wine and chocolate, and the texture is smooth and velvety.

Serves 4

* **1 litre açai pulp, fresh or defrosted**
* **150g black treacle**
* **1 tsp salt**

1. In a large bowl, combine the açai pulp, molasses and salt using a wire whisk. Place in the freezer.

2. When the mixture is well chilled, transfer to an ice cream machine and churn the sorbet following the manufacturer's instructions.

Tips from Thiago:
This sorbet is also delicious when you substitute honey for the black treacle. If you do not have an ice cream machine, follow the tip opposite.

Sorvete de doce de leite com cumaru e flor de sal

Dulce de leche ice cream with tonka bean and sea salt

Serves 8

* **3 egg yolks**
* **2 tbsp dark muscovado sugar**
* **900ml double cream**
* **500g dulce de leche**
* **1 tbsp grated tonka bean or seeds from 1 vanilla pod**
* **1 tbsp sea salt flakes**

1. Whisk the egg yolks and muscovado sugar together in a heatproof bowl for 3 minutes or until the mixture is slightly pale. Set aside.

2. In a saucepan, combine the cream, dulce de leche and tonka bean. Bring to a simmer over a very low heat and cook for 5 minutes.

3. Remove from the heat and, being careful not to get burned, pour this scalding mixture over the eggs and sugar, whisking constantly.

4. When the mixture is well combined, pour it back into the saucepan. Simmer gently for a further 4 minutes over a very low heat, stirring constantly with the whisk to prevent the egg yolks curdling.

5. Remove the caramel custard from the heat, strain it into a bowl and refrigerate for 1 hour or until cold.

6. Fold the sea salt flakes into the chilled custard using a wooden spoon, then transfer to an ice cream machine and churn following the manufacturer's instructions.

Tips from Thiago:

If you do not have an ice cream machine, follow the tip on page 238.

Sorbet de chocolate do Combu

Combu chocolate sorbet

This sorbet reaches perfection when the chocolate is pure, made without sugar, milk or other typical additions. At Remanso do Bosque, we are fortunate to have access to Combu Island chocolate. This is handmade by our dear Nena, an artisan who devotes her life to manufacturing a product that, for us, is synonymous with poetry.

Serves 4

* **185g caster sugar**
* **30g cocoa powder**
* **185g chocolate, 100% cocoa solids**
* **30g cocoa nibs**

1. Put the sugar in a medium saucepan with 500ml of water. Cook, stirring, over a low heat for 3 minutes or until the sugar has dissolved. Remove the pan from the heat, mix in the cocoa powder and set aside.

2. Chop the chocolate and melt in a double boiler. Remove the top pan from the heat and, a little at a time, pour in the warm cocoa syrup, stirring constantly with a wire whisk until well combined.

3. Cool the mixture immediately by dipping the bottom of the pan into a bowl filled with ice cubes and a little cold water. Stir well until cool.

4. Fold in the cocoa nibs, then refrigerate so that the mixture is well chilled. Transfer to an ice cream machine and churn following the manufacturer's instructions.

Tips from Thiago:

If you do not have an ice cream machine, follow the tip on page 238.

Sorbet de manga com gengibre
Mango and ginger sorbet

Serves 8

* **120g caster sugar**
* **900g ripe mango flesh, preferably Palmer, chopped**
* **60ml lime juice**
* **40g root ginger, peeled and chopped**

1. Put the sugar in a medium saucepan with 250ml water and place over a low heat. Stir until the sugar dissolves completely then increase the heat and cook for 4 minutes. Set aside to cool.

2. Process the mango, lime juice, ginger and syrup in a blender for 4 minutes or until the mixture is smooth. Pass through a sieve and refrigerate for 1 hour.

3. Transfer the chilled mixture to an ice cream machine and churn the sorbet following the manufacturer's instructions.

Tips from Thiago:

If you do not have an ice cream machine, follow the tip on page 238.

Sorbet de banana--da-terra com limão
Plantain and lime sorbet

Serves 5

* **600g ripe plantains, unpeeled**
* **30ml lime juice**
* **30g glucose syrup**
* **150g caster sugar**

1. Preheat the oven to 180°C (350°F), gas mark 4. Put the unpeeled plantains on a baking tray and bake for 30 minutes until very soft.

2. When cool enough to handle, peel the plantains and put the flesh in a blender. Add the lime juice and blend to a smooth cream. Leave the mixture in the blender jug and set aside.

3. Put the glucose syrup and caster sugar in a saucepan with 400ml of water and bring to the boil over a low heat, stirring until the sugar has dissolved. Cook for 3 minutes, then remove from the heat and leave to cool.

4. Pour the syrup into the plantain cream and blend until completely smooth. Churn in an ice cream maker, following the manufacturer's instructions.

Tips from Thiago:

If you do not have an ice cream machine, follow the tip on page 238.

Brazil is the world's largest coffee producer and the second largest consumer of the beverage, and the state of Minas Gerais produces 51.4 per cent of Brazil's production.

In 2011, Bruno Souza, the fourth generation of a family of coffee producers, opened Academia do Café, featuring a laboratory, workshop and training centre for tasters, baristas and coffee graders. Today Academia do Café is known nationally and throughout the world, and Bruno has become one of the most respected coffee experts anywhere.

Academia do Café is a small but exceptional company fully dedicated to coffee culture and prepares exclusive coffee blends for restaurants and coffee lovers. The beans are carefully roasted and packed with great dedication, resulting in products that are 100 per cent artisanal and unique.

KEY INGREDIENTS

AÇAÍ – the fruit of the assai/açai palm (*Euterpe oleracea*), the thick pulp of which is widely consumed by the riverside populations of the Amazon. It is served as an accompaniment to savoury dishes, especially fish, and has an intense blueberry-like flavour. Also considered a 'super fruit', it is used nowadays as a highly nutritious ingredient, often consumed in smoothies or with added sugar, fresh fruit and granola. For cooking, buy frozen açai berry pulp from Brazilian or Asian shops; it is also available online from specialist açaí suppliers.

ANNATTO – a plant (*Bixa orellana*) widely used across the Americas, annatto (achiote) was one of the primitive components of chocolate of the Aztecs. Used by Brazilian natives to paint their skin and to impart colour and flavour to their food as well, it can be found in oil and powder form.

AVIÚ – a minute crustacean (*Acetes americanus*), similar to shrimp, that lives in the mouth of the Amazon Basin rivers, especially in the Tapajós. It has an intense flavour, and is sold dried and salted for use in cooking.

BACURI – one of the most important Amazon fruits (*Platonia insignis*), much appreciated for its aroma and delicate acidity, it has a white pulp that results in excellent ice cream, jellies, juice and desserts. Buy the frozen pulp in Brazilian stores.

BEIJU – similar to a crepe, it is made with moistened cassava starch and served with different fillings in a number of dishes. It is essentially the cassava flatbread.

BRAZIL NUTS – known in Brazil as castanha-do-pará ('Pará nuts'), they are the fruit of a type of chestnut tree, the only species in the genus Bertholletia. Cultivated for millennia by the native peoples of the Amazon region, these nuts are considered the finest in Brazil. They are usually consumed roasted.

BRAZIL NUT MILK – extracted from raw Brazil nuts (see page 116), this is very common in the north region.

BREADFRUIT – fruit of a large tree (*Artocarpus incisa L*) of Asian origin and introduced into Brazil in the 18th century. Its pulp and seeds are used in baking and desserts. You can buy the fresh fruit from African and Asian stores and market stalls.

CALABRESA – smoked sausage made with diced pork and fat seasoned with red pepper flakes (pimenta calabresa in Portuguese).

CAMURIM – a native Tupi language word to designate the white snook (*Centropomus undecimalis*), a fish that can be found off the coast of the Americas. The white flesh has a delicate flavour and a flaky texture.

CARANGUEJO – OR CARANGUEJO-UÇÁ (*Ucides cordatus*) is a mangrove crab, typical of the Pará state. The cooked and shredded meat is the basic ingredient of casquinha de caranguejo, Brazilian-style dressed crab, served in its shell, with added local seasonings and farofa.

CARIMÃ – also called mandioca mole ('soft cassava'), this is cassava root pulp left to soak in water to ferment. The fermented paste yields various preparations, including farinha de carimã, which is a finer, whiter and more delicate cassava flour, used to prepare porridge of various kinds. European settlers often used this flour to replace wheat flour.

CARNE DE SOL – literally 'sun meat', and also called carne de vento ('wind meat') and carne do sertão ('backland meat'), it consists of pieces (called mantas, 'blankets') or strips of salted air-dried meat. It has a shorter shelf life than carne seca, as it is cured with less salt.

CARNE SECA – also known as charque. It has several other names in Portuguese, including jabá and carne-do-Rio-Grande. The beef is boned and cut into large pieces (called mantas, 'blankets'), which are salted and dried in the sun, and then stacked. The same process was used throughout Spanish America during colonization.

CASHEW FRUIT – also called cashew apple in English, it is the false fruit of a tree (*Anacardium occidentale*) characterized by an unmistakably unique astringency, aroma and flavour. The cashew 'nut' (which is the actual fruit, and hangs outside on the bottom part of the 'apple') is widely consumed in Brazil and elsewhere, usually roasted.

CASSAVA ROOT – see **macaxeira**.

CHARQUE – see **carne seca**.

CHICÓRIA-DO-PARÁ – a herb (*Eryngium foetidum l.*) with several popular names, both in English (including culantro, and Mexican or long, spiny and serrated coriander) and in Portuguese (including coentro-de-peixe, -de-pasto, -de-chão and coentrão). It has become widely known in Brazil because of its use in Pará cuisine, where it is one of the most popular herbs. Coriander is a suitable substitute because the flavour is similar; however, the texture of chicória-do-Pará is more like romaine lettuce.

COLORAU – powdered seasoning made with cornmeal, saturated with the natural oil released by annatto (achiote) seeds.

CUMARI-DO-PARÁ CHILLI – a variety of **pimenta-de-cheiro** from the genus *Capsicum chinense Jacquin*, which is very common in the Amazon region. It has an oval shape and a light yellow colour. It can be eaten raw, pickled in vinegar or in oil and is an essential ingredient in several dishes of the north region of Brazil.

CUMARU – an Amazonian tree (*Dipteryx odorata*) bearing very aromatic seeds, known in English as tonka beans. They have medicinal uses in the Amazon and are used in cooking elsewhere, too, often replacing vanilla.

CUPUAÇU – from the same family as the cacao, the fruit of this tree (*Theobroma grandiflorum*) is consumed fresh and used in desserts. More recently, in the modern Brazilian kitchen, it has been making its way into savoury dishes as well. The pulp has a sweet-and-sour flavour and a distinct aroma, reminiscent of ether. You can buy it frozen in Brazilian, African and Asian stores. Sometimes the fresh fruit is available at Asian market stalls.

DENDÊ – also called azeite de dendê or palm oil. It is extracted from the fruit of a palm tree (*Elaeis guineensis*), originally from Africa, and widely used in Bahian cooking (see Bahia-style Fish Stew, page 134) as well as in the religious cooking of the Recôncavo Baiano. Easy to find in large supermarkets, dendê is yellow-orange in colour and has a strong flavour. It's smoking point is 230°C, which is high compared to many oils commonly used for frying.

FARINHA-D'ÁGUA – a crunchy, acidic-tasting flour made by leaving cassava roots soaking in water for several days to ferment and soften before processing, which includes grating, squeezing, drying and toasting over a hot, dry surface.

FARINHA DE CARIMÃ – see **carimã**.

FARINHA DE MANDIOCA – flour obtained from the dried fibre of fresh cassava roots after they are rinsed, peeled, grated and pressed. It is the most widely used by-product of cassava in all parts of Brazil, and the flour is available raw or toasted. An ingredient of **farofa** and **pirão**, it is also used to sprinkle on top of stewed beans, poultry, meat or fish. Raw cassava flour and polvilho (see **goma de mandioca**) are the most important ones to buy when you are first trying your hand at Brazilian cooking.

FARINHA DE SURUÍ – a traditional, fine-grained cassava flour of Pará. Its name refers to the ethnicity of the local Suruí natives. The texture is a little crunchy and the taste is similar to toasted cassava flour.

FARINHA DE TAPIOCA – a product obtained through the partial conversion of cassava starch by heating the moistened starch on a hot griddle. The starch coagulates, forming round, lightweight granules that look like tiny balls of foam. This 'flour' has no particular flavour but absorbs the flavour of other ingredients; texture is its most important quality. Farinha de tapioca is extensively used in Pará to accompany açaí pulp, as well as in many savoury and sweet preparations. Sold outside Brazil as 'tapioca' under the Yoki brand. Compare with **tapioca granulada**.

FAROFA – a dry mixture of toasted cassava flour or farinha de milho (Brazilian flaked cornmeal) and seasonings such as garlic, onion, bacon, parsley, eggs, sausage, etc. It is used as an accompaniment for meat, fish or poultry. A sweet mixture with the same appearance and texture is served with desserts.

FEIJÃO-ANDÚ – known as pigeon peas in English, this small green legume is of the genus *Cajanus cajan*, which is bushy and not trailing, like other beans. Widely consumed in the northeast of Brazil, its varieties can be found throughout the country. It has a creamy texture when cooked.

FEIJÃO-MANTEIGUINHA – a variety of *Phaseolus vulgaris*, probably developed by artificial selection. It can be found in lowland crops throughout the Amazon River. Beans from the most famous location (the town of Santarém in Pará state) have been used in gourmet cooking in recent years. They are small, brown and have a firm texture that remains al dente when cooked.

FILHOTE – (literally 'little one'), so called because it is a smaller version of the largest freshwater fish in the world, the piraíba (*Brachyplathystoma filamentosum*), a type of catfish that reaches 300kg. The name filhote is used for fish of up to 60kg. One of the major components of the Amazonian diet, it has a firm, white, very delicate flesh. The belly is fatty but the rest of the fish is lean.

FUBÁ – fine flour obtained by milling dry corn.

GOMA DE MANDIOCA – cassava starch freshly extracted from roots after they have been ground and squeezed. The remaining mass is passed through a sieve and used in this form to make several dishes, such as **beiju** and tacacá (see recipe on page 56). It can also be fermented and dried to make **polvilho azedo**, simply dried to make **polvilho doce**, or dried and toasted to make **farinha de mandioca** and **farinha de tapioca**.

GUARIMÃ – a plant (*Ischnosiphon arouma; Marantaceae*) that produces fibres for clothing and artifacts. The tipiti, a piece of native Brazilian equipment used to squeeze the liquid out of the cassava pulp during the preparation of tucupi, is made of guarimã fibres; the fresh leaves of the plant are also used in cooking and have similar qualities to banana leaves.

HEARTS OF PALM – also known as palm hearts. See **pupunha** and page 170).

JABOTICABA – a plant of the *Myrtaceae* family, originating in the Atlantic forest, it bears fruit that are attached directly to the tree trunk. It has an extremely delicate pulp and astringent skin. The flavour is reminiscent of cassis, and the fruit is widely used to make juice, jellies and sorbets.

JACKFRUIT – the fruit of a tree (*Artocarpus heterophyllus*) originating in India and introduced into Brazil by the Portuguese at the beginning of colonization. It has a distinct, sweet aroma and a fibrous starchy texture. The flavour can be compared to a combination of banana and pineapple.

JAMBO-VERMELHO – a fruit known as red water pear in English, it comes from a particular tree of the *Myrtaceae* family (*Syzygium malaccense*) which has several species. Especially appreciated raw, this fragrant variety has a rose-like flavour and the texture of a hard pear.

JAMBU – a herb (*Acmella oleracea*), typical of the Amazon, known in English by several names (including Pará cress, Pará or Amazon watercress, and toothache plant), it has the appearance of a wild watercress and temporarily numbs the senses in the mouth when chewed. The leaves and flowers are used in several dishes of Pará cuisine.

MACAXEIRA – the same as **mandioca** and aipim, it is an edible plant variety (*Manihot utilissima*), known as mandioca mansa (literally 'tame cassava'), with low levels of hydrocyanic acid, with different names in some regions of Brazil. The roots of the plant are used in the production of the most popular flour in Brazil, cassava flour, and several other by-products; the fibrous, bitter-tasting leaves are used to make **maniva**.

MANDIOCA – see **macaxeira**.

MANDIOQUINHA – also called batata baroa and batata salsa in Portuguese, this root vegetable is known in English as arracacha and Peruvian parsnip, and in French as pomme de terre-céleri. It is used to make purées and soups, its deep yellow flesh having a consistency similar to cooked cassava. However, it is not as starchy, and the flavour is sweeter and more delicate.

MANIVA – the Brazilian name for the stem of the cassava plant and also for cassava leaves, which are the key ingredient in Maniçoba (see page 46).

MANTEIGA DE GARRAFA – yellowish, viscous fat from cows' milk that is similar to clarified butter and ghee.

MAXIXE – a plant of the cucurbit family originating in Africa, known in English as West Indian gherkin, among other names. It is very popular in the back land of the Northeast region of Brazil. Its flavour is reminiscent of cucumber, and it can be used in many preparations, from salads to stews.

MINIARROZ (or Mini Arroz) – a small rice variety that was developed by artificial selection in the Paraíba Valley, in the State of São Paulo, Brazil.

MOQUECA – see pages 134 and 138.

PAÇOCA – see page 90.

PACU – an oily freshwater fish with more than 20 species, including the piranha and the tambaqui, it is commonly found in the Amazon basin and is much appreciated for its flavour. Pacu is small and flat and generally no larger than 800g.

PAIO – a sausage of Portuguese origin made with pork and spices, a required ingredient of feijoada.

PALMITO – the Portuguese word for **hearts of palm** or palm hearts.

PEACH PALM FRUIT – the fruit of a palm tree that can grow up to 20 metres tall and is very common in the lowland areas of the Amazon. It is called **pupunha** in Portuguese; the natives enjoy both the nut and the flesh of the fruit – with its striking yellow colour and remarkable nutty flavour. You can sometimes find it fresh in African and Asian shops.

PEQUI – the fruit of a tree (*Caryocar brasiliense*) widespread in Brazil from southeast to north. The edible golden-yellow flesh has unparalleled taste and aroma, and produces an oil, azeite de pequi, which can be used as a condiment. It is used in traditional preparations, usually containing rice and chicken, or to make liqueur. It can be bought fresh, preserved in brine or as a paste.

PESCADA AMARELA – a saltwater fish (*Cynoscion acoupa*) known in English as acoupa weakfish, it can reach up to 1 metre in length and is considered a superior fish because of the excellent quality of its flaky flesh. In Pará, it lives in the brackish water where the river meets the sea; this imparts a special minerally flavour to its flesh.

PIMENTA BIQUINHO – called kiss pepper in English, it is a variety developed by hybridization in a public institution in the state of Minas Gerais. These small round peppers are either scarlet red or sunshine-yellow and readily identifiable by the small beak-shaped protuberance hanging at the end. The flavour is aromatic and juicy but not spicy. You can find them sold in jars in Brazilian stores.

PIMENTA DEDO-DE-MOÇA – a red chilli of the genus *Capsicum baccatum Pendulum*. It is comparatively mild at 5,000-15,000 Scoville units and widely consumed all over Brazil, in preserved and fresh forms.

PIMENTA MALAGUETA – the bird's-eye chilli, also known by its Portuguese name piri piri. Widely used in Brazilian and African cuisines, it is not excessively hot, and can be preserved in oil or vinegar or ground into a powder.

PIMENTA-DE-CHEIRO – the common name for numerous varieties of chilli (*Capsicum odoriferum*), with different colours and shapes, all characterized by low piquancy and strong aroma. They are widely used in the cuisine of Brazil's north. See also **cumari-do-Pará chilli**.

PIRACUÍ – dried fish flour made from moqueado fish (dried on a rack positioned over a campfire, but not too close to the heat and the smoke). It is shredded and pounded until reduced almost to a powder, and then sifted. Normally part of the provisions for long journeys, it can also be used as an ingredient in other dishes, such as stews and fried appetizers.

PIRÃO – a mixture of cassava flour and water or other flavourful liquid, cooked to the consistency of a thin porridge and served as an accompaniment to fish and occasionally to chicken and meat.

PIRARUCU – the *Arapaima gigas*, known in English as arapaima, is the largest fish with scales in the world and can reach 200kg. It was used by the Portuguese as a substitute for cod, salt-cured in large pieces (called mantas, 'blankets') that could be stored for long periods of time.

PLANTAIN – called banana-da-terra ('banana of the land') in Portuguese and pacova by the native Indians. It is used in a multitude of dishes, mostly cooked or baked.

POLVILHO AZEDO / DOCE – see **goma de mandioca**.

PRATIQUEIRA – the name of a very common class of oily fish (*Mugil curema Valenciennes*) with 18 different species, widely consumed in Pará. The flavour is strongly salty.

PUPUNHA – the Portuguese word for a sustainable type of hearts of palm extracted from the peach palm tree. The fruit of that tree is also called pupunha. See **peach palm fruit**.

PUXURI – a plant of the Laurel family (*Ocotea besthamiana*), it is a tree native to the Amazon rainforest that produces a very aromatic seed, resembling a mixture of nutmeg and star anise. Widely used in teas in Britain as early as the 18th century, today it is being increasingly used in cooking as well.

QUEIJO DA CANASTRA MEIA-CURA – cheese from the region of Serra da Canastra, in Minas Gerais. It is regarded as the most prestigious in the country, and is probably derived from Portugal's São Jorge cheese, from the Azores, during the colonial period.

QUEIJO DE COALHO – popular in Brazil, this cheese is made from raw cows' milk and has a semi-hard consistency.

QUEIJO DO MARAJÓ – cooked curd cheese similar in its manufacture to mozzarella. It is made from buffalo milk on the island of Marajó, where buffalo farming is a tradition.

RAPADURA – the name given to sugar produced from the juice of sugarcane, boiled until thickened and then poured into rectangular boxes to dry. It is usually sold in bars, which can be cut and eaten as a type of hard fudge, or grated to be used in recipes or as a sweetener. Health food stores around the world sell it as an alternative type of sugar.

SARNABI – also called sarnambi, this is a type of clam (*Phacoides pectinatus*), known in Portugal as almeijôa, and as vongola in Italy.

TAMBAQUI – a fish with scales of the Amazon River basin of the species *Colossoma macropomum*. It has a firm, fatty meat similar to pork and is much appreciated by the riverbank peoples.

TAPIOCA GRANULADA – a type of flour, derived from cassava, that has the appearance of broken tapioca pearls. Also called tapioca quebrada and farinha de tapioca in some regions of the country. However, in Pará (and therefore in this book) this term refers to a 'flour' that has granules similar to tiny balls of foam (compare with **farinha de tapioca**).

TUCUPI – a yellow liquid of indigenous origins. It is prepared by cooking the liquid extracted from ground cassava root during the preparation of flour. There are three types of tucupi: boiled, evaporated and black. The first of these types is most common and seasoned with **pimenta-de-cheiro**, **chicória-do-Pará** and garlic (see substitute recipe on page 104.)

VINAGREIRA – a plant of the Hibiscus family (*Hibiscus sabdariffa*) the leaves of which are used in recipes such as arroz de cuxá, a typical dish of the dtate of Maranhão, eaten with dried salt shrimp. The flavour is sour.

USEFUL ADDRESSES

Remanso do Bosque
Chef: Thiago Castanho
Av. Rômulo Maiorana com Perebebuí – Marco
Belém/PA
www.restauranteremanso.com.br

Remanso do Peixe
Chef: Seu Chicão
Barão do Triunfo, 66093-050 Belém/PA
www.restauranteremanso.com.br

Mocotó – Restaurante e Cachaçaria
Chef: Rodrigo Oliveira
Av. Ns. do Loreto, 1100 – Vila Medeiros, São Paulo/SP
www.mocoto.com.br

Bar da Dona Onça
Chef: Janaina Rueda
Av. Ipiranga, 200 – República, São Paulo/SP
www.bardadonaonca.com.br

Lagundri
Chef: Marcelo Amaral
Saldanha Marinho, 1061, Centro, Curitiba/PR
www.lagundri.com.br

Restaurant Durski & Restaurant Madero
Chef: Junior Durski
Av. Jaime Reis, 254, São Francisco, Curitiba/PR
www.durski.com.br
& www.restaurantemadero.com.br/prime

Roberta Sudbrack
Chef: Roberta Sudbrack
Av. Lineu de Paula Machado, 916
Jardim Botânico, Rio de Janeiro/RJ
www.robertasudbrack.com.br

Trindade
Chefs: Felipe Rameh & Fred Trindade
Rua Alvarenga Peixoto, 388, Belo Horizonte/MG
www.trindadebrasil.com.br

Gotazkaen Estúdio
Artist: Daniel Zuil
Rua Ó de Almeida, 755, Belém/PA
www.gotaz.com.br

Casa d'Noca
Owners: Luciana Fajardo & Flávia Anjos
Av. 9 de Janeiro, 1677 – São Brás, Belém/PA
www.casadnoca.com

Academia do Café
Owner: Bruno Souza
Avenida do Contorno, 4.392, Funcionários, Belo Horizonte/MG
www.academiadocafe.com.br

Casa do Barreado
Owner: Lindamar Santos Silva
Rua Isidoro Costa Pinto, 496, Centro, Antonina/PR

WHERE TO BUY BRAZILIAN INGREDIENTS

Casa Brasil
23–25 Queensway
London W2 4QJ
020 7792 2931

Brazilian Emporium
Station Offices
Station Road
London NW10 4UX
020 8965 6058

Mercearia Brasil
773 Harrow Road
London NW10 5PA
020 8962 0252

For fruits & vegetables

Brixton Village
Coldharbour Lane
London SW9 8PS
020 7274 2990

Brixton Market
Atlantic Road
London SW9 8JB
020 7274 2990

Longdan
4 Estate Way
London E10 7JN
020 8556 8828

FLK Chinese Groceries
3 Station Buildings
Catford Road
London SE6 4QZ
020 8690 0898

For meat

Acougue Ki Carne
24 Station Road
London NW10 4UE
020 8961 2600

Boi Gordo Butchers
223 Mare Street
London E8 3QE
020 8986 6215

Casa de Carnes Brasil
1096 Harrow Road
London NW10 5NL
020 8964 3034

Online retailers:
www.casabrasillondres.co.uk
www.supermercadoportugal.com
www.produtosbrasileiros.co.uk
www.afrocaribbeanstore.co.uk
www.africanonestopshop.co.uk
www.pulpastore.co.uk
www.sublimefood.co.uk

Índice } Index

I would like to thank my father, my mother, my brother and my whole team at the Remanso restaurants who are really part of my family.

Many thanks, too, to the people who inspire me, including Nena, Beth Cheirosinha, Cavalo, Neneca, Dona Dijé, Noemi Porro, Marinaldo Santos and Daniel Silva.

I dedicate this book especially to the diners who come to my restaurants and believe in our work.

Thiago

I would like to thank Elisa and Iain – without you this book would not have been possible. And Ivo and Dória, who offered their support, knowledge and friendship.

To all invited chefs, thank you for so kindly sharing your recipes with us.

To the Castanho family, who became my family in Pará – this book pays homage to you, Chicão and Carmem!

Many thanks go to Lu and Flávia, of the Casa d'Noca, and Cris, Pascal and Luiz Paulo, Nilson (our king of the ribs!), to Marcelo and Sandra (the laser beam couple!), to the family and friends of the Remanso do Bosque restaurants, and the beautiful people of Ver-o-Peso.

Finally, my special thanks go to my dear Clive and Julie, for their patience, love and support during my numerous and prolonged absences.

Luciana